RITUAL ABUSE AND
MIND CONTROL

RITUAL ABUSE AND MIND CONTROL

The Manipulation of Attachment Needs

Edited by

Orit Badouk Epstein, Joseph Schwartz,
and Rachel Wingfield Schwartz

The Bowlby Centre

KARNAC

Published in 2011 by
Karnac Books Ltd
118 Finchley Road, London NW3 5HT

British Library Cataloguing in Publication Data

A C.I.P. for this book is available from the British Library

ISBN: 978 1 85575 839 1

Edited, designed and produced by The Studio Publishing Services Ltd
www.publishingservicesuk.co.uk
e-mail: studio@publishingservicesuk.co.uk

Printed in Great Britain

www.karnacbooks.com

CONTENTS

ACKNOWLEDGEMENTS

Thanks and appreciation to the Conference organizing group: Natasha Roffe, Briony Mason, Elizabeth London, and Orit Badouk Epstein, for the skill, passion, and generosity they brought to producing this pioneering conference. It was a remarkable experience to work in the context of so much warmth, courage, and solidarity, never undermined by the traumatic nature of the material we were working on together.

A very special thank you needs to go to Valerie Sinason and the Clinic for Dissociative Studies, who jointly hosted the conference. Without Valerie, no psychotherapy conference on this subject would ever have been held.

Many thanks to the Executive of The Bowlby Centre, who had the integrity and political strength to back a conference on this issue and to associate the Centre's name publicly with the treatment of ritual abuse survivors.

Our heartfelt thanks also go to Oliver Rathbone for his willingness to publish a book which is not only ground-breaking, but also controversial, and for his continuing commitment to giving a voice to writers in the fields of attachment and trauma.

Last, and most importantly, we would like to acknowledge the survivors of ritual abuse and mind control who have refused to be silenced and whose capacity to fight back in the face of extreme torture teaches every one of us what we need to understand about the human spirit—that love is stronger than hate. We dedicate this book to them.

Rachel Wingfield Schwartz

Anonymous is a survivor of organized ritual abuse, torture, and mind control, and a writer, campaigner, international speaker, and trainer specializing in psychosis and trauma.

Orit Badouk Epstein is an attachment-based psychoanalytic psychotherapist and supervisor who trained at The Bowlby Centre, London where she is a member of the executive committee. She runs a private practice in North London and is one of the trustees of the Paracelsus Trust at the Clinic for Dissociative Studies. Orit has an interest in, and experience of, working with clients who have suffered from extensive trauma and abuse, including ritual abuse, sexual abuse, violence, and emotional abuse. Orit has published articles in the Attachment Journal and is on the editorial board of the ESTD news letter. She is committed to campaigns to counteract the denial and disbelief around Ritual Abuse. Email: orit_badouk@hotmail.com

Ellen Lacter has been a clinical psychologist in California, USA for the past twenty-three years, and has specialized in the treatment of dissociative disorders and ritual abuse and mind control trauma in both children and adults for the past twelve years. She has a number of published chapters in edited books on the subject of ritual abuse and mind control. She is programme co-ordinator for the Play Therapy Certificate Program at University of California San Diego-Extension. She is also an activist on behalf of victims of ritual abuse and mind control, and maintains a website to educate the public and mental health community on these subjects: http://www.endritualabuse.org/

Sue Richardson is a member of The Bowlby Centre with over thirty years' experience in the helping professions. Her personal and professional attachment networks are in the northeast of England, from where she provides training, consultation, and supervision for those working with complex trauma and dissociation. Sue is a member of the European Society for Trauma and Dissociation (ESTD) and the International Society for the Study of Dissociation (ISSTD), and a founder member of their UK networks. She belongs to the training faculty of ISSTD and is the Training Co-ordinator for ESTD UK. She is the co-editor and co-author of two books and a number of published papers concerning child abuse trauma, attachment, and dissociation. suerichardson1@compuserve.com

Joseph Schwartz is a training therapist and supervisor at the Bowlby Centre. His books include *Cassandra's Daughter: A History of Psychoanalysis in Europe and America* (Penguin & Karnac). He is the author of numerous papers on clinical practice, the history of psychoanalysis, and the role of genetics in mental distress. josephschwartz@btinternet.com

Valerie Sinason is a poet, writer, child and adult psychoanalytic psychotherapist, and adult psychoanalyst. She is Director of the Clinic for Dissociative Studies, Honorary Consultant Psychotherapist for Cape Town Child Guidance Clinic, and President of the Institute for Psychotherapy and Disability. She has been a Consultant at the Tavistock and Portman Clinics until 1998, when she left to start the Clinic for Dissociative Studies. She has also been a Consultant Research Psychotherapist at St George's Hospital Medical School. She specializes in trauma, disability, abuse, and dissociation. In 1994, she published *Treating Survivors of Satanist Abuse* (Routledge) as a result of a Department of Health funded clinical piece of research carried out at the Portman Clinic. Her most recent book, *Attachment, Trauma and Multiplicity* (Routledge), is coming out in a revised edition next year. vsinason@aol.com

Rachel Wingfield Schwartz is a UKCP Registered Psychotherapist and was the Chair of the Bowlby Centre 2002–2009 (formerly Centre for Attachment-based Psychoanalytic Psychotherapy), where she is also a training supervisor and teacher. Rachel has a wide range of clinical experience in a variety of settings, including schools and prisons, and specializes in working with survivors of trauma and abuse, including sexual abuse, rape, domestic violence, war, state terror, and ritual and cult abuse. Rachel has been working with ritual abuse survivors since 1993 and is passionately committed to ending the disbelief and silence surrounding this issue. Rachel is also a psychotherapist with the Clinic for Dissociative Studies. rachelwingfield@btinternet.com

Introduction

Joseph Schwartz

Twenty years ago I first heard Valerie Sinason describe her work with victims of ritual abuse. The cost to her was enormous. She could scarcely believe any of things she was told, the tortures and the horrifying involvement of trusted pillars of the community—doctors, lawyers, police. It was Rosemary's Baby in spades. Valerie was terrified.

I did know from Valerie's work with mental handicap the kinds of abuse that can be perpetuated by those in power over the vulnerable, including the continuous reports of abuse perpetrated in old age homes, in the Catholic Church, and in the cellars of madmen like Josef Fritzl. But ritual abuse seemed a step too far.

I felt myself rebelling at the words satanic abuse. What? In this day and age people believe in Satan? Surely not. But, actually, horrifying as it was, I had little trouble seeing ritual abuse more simply as organized abuse. After all, in the USA, people organize themselves into lynching parties, the kind of terror that had never been far away during my time in Mississippi. I was further helped by one survivor saying, "Satanic abuse, Schmatanic abuse. What is going on here is torture."

Abu Ghraib, the Maze Prison in Northern Ireland, the School of the Americas in Fort Benning, Georgia, where Latin American police forces are trained in the techniques of torture: we are surrounded by examples of torture. Dr Sheila Cassidy testified eloquently to the torture she endured at the hands of Chilean police during the coup against Allende (Cassidy, 1977). Bobby Sands starved himself to death in protest at torture at the Maze Prison in Northern Ireland. John Schlapobursky has turned his torture at the hands of the South African police into lifelong work with trauma survivors here in London.

The images of torture at Abu Ghraib prison by the US army will stay etched in our minds for many years (see The Abu Ghraib Prison Photos, Google Images). So why shouldn't rogue elements in our communities, often, indeed, pillars of our communities, organize themselves into rings to do with children what they please, including torture and mind control to prevent the torture from being disclosed?

In the present case of the torture of children, where are the techniques learnt that are so necessary to keep the victims silenced? The CIA's MKUltra documents (thousands of papers and articles on which are listed on Google and can be found at Declassified MK-Ultra Project Documents) on mind control are discussed by Ellen Lacter in her fine chapter. The question asked by MKUltra experimenters was: "Can we get control of an individual to the point where he will do our bidding against his will and even against such fundamental laws of nature as self-preservation?" (MKULTRA, 1952). The experiments are hair-raising. You can see a fictional representation of the techniques used in the last of the Bourne films, *The Bourne Ultimatum*. Director Paul Greengrass has done his homework to show the use of torture (waterboarding) to create manipulatable, altered self-states. Remember, fiction tells us stories that are valuable and true. We do have non-fiction sources to back this up. Ellen Lacter, in this volume, documents the gory details of torture-based mind control.

*   *   *

We are fully aware that ritual abuse is an extremely controversial subject with a particularly aggressive and vociferous opposition. The crude, sadistic satires in *Private Eye* (Anon, 2010) are the least of it. The substance of the attacks on the reality of organized abuse and torture of children always reduce to that old chestnut—it is unscientific. "Give us proof," say the naysayers. "How is this different from reports of alien abduction?" say the clever-clever wags of *Private Eye*.

Indeed. How is it different? In the case of alien abduction, we are asked to believe that visitors to this planet from outer space have kidnapped someone, taken them away, and brought them back. It is not believable. In the case of ritual abuse, we are asked to believe that people can organize themselves into groups for the purpose of torturing children. There would seem to be a significant difference here in what we are asked to believe.

But we are dealing with belief systems. Belief systems resist change, sometimes vociferously and aggressively. Consider, for example, Holocaust deniers. This extreme form of anti-Semitism believes that the Holocaust is a Jewish propaganda coup. "... historians have a blindness when it comes to the Holocaust because like Tay-Sachs disease it is a Jewish disease which causes blindness" (Irving, 1986).

What is the belief system behind the aggressive vociferous denials of ritual abuse torture? I believe that this is a refusal/incapacity to see/entertain just how brutal our social system has been and is. Check out the nineteenth-century images of child labour (Google Images: Child labour, nineteenth-century Britain). Until recently, our culture has always brutalized its children (DeMause, 1995). But in my experience, no amount of evidence can defeat a belief system. No matter what evidence is offered, there will always be vociferous and aggressive denial of the reality of ritual abuse torture or, as history of psychoanalysis shows, the reality of childhood sexual abuse, full stop. The case of Holocaust deniers is just one extreme example of aggressive denial.

Readers picking up this book will want to evaluate the evidence for themselves. In this effort they may well be deterred by the argument that the evidence is not objective or, in the argument's more abusive form, the evidence is unscientific.

What does "unscientific" really mean?

When evidence is labelled "unscientific", it means it is not to be trusted. And vice versa. To be scientific means to be trusted, as in the advertising trope, "It is a scientific fact that . . ." What is the adjective "scientific" doing in there? What, really, after all, is a "scientific" fact? A fact is a fact. Or, as my father used to say, "Facts are stubborn things." (And, mind you, facts are socially constructed by human labour (Fleck, 1979).)

Psychoanalysis has suffered the accusation of being "unscientific" from its very beginnings (Schwartz, 1999). In recent years, the Berkeley literary critic Frederick Crews has renewed the assault on the talking cure in verbose, unreadable articles in the *New York Review of Books* (Crews, 1990), inevitably concluding, because nothing else really persuades, that psychoanalysis fails because it is unscientific. The chorus was joined by philosopher of science, Adolf Grunbaum (1985), who played both ends against the middle: to the philosophers he professed specialist knowledge of psychoanalysis; to the psychoanalysts he professed specialist knowledge of science, particularly physics. Neither was true (Schwartz, 1995a,b, 1996a,b, 2000).

The problem that mental health clinicians always face is that we deal with human subjectivity in a culture that is deeply invested in denying the importance of human subjectivity. Freud's great invention of the analytic hour allows us to explore, with our clients, their inner worlds. Can such a subjective instrument be trusted? Not by very many. It is so dangerously close to women's intuition. So-called objectivity is the name of the game in our culture. Nevertheless, 100 years of clinical practice have shown psychoanalysis and psychotherapy not only to be effective, but to yield real understandings of the dynamics of human relationships, particularly the reality of transference–countertransference re-enactments now reformulated by our neuroscientists as right brain to right brain communication (Schore, 1999).

*   *   *

I think there is danger that the politics of ritual abuse and mind control, particularly the involvement of our State apparatus in its development and practice, can deflect us from proper concern with survivors. This book is a report from a powerful, moving conference where, for the first time, a safe enough space had been created for survivors and therapists to come together to discuss the pain and difficulties of recovering from the torture of ritual abuse and mind control. This book is a tribute to those victims who have had the courage to come forward and tell us what they have had to survive. It has taken courage because we, as potential witnesses, can become hostile and rejecting in hearing about crimes of this nature. Each case is a mini-Holocaust of torture. Like the Nazis, the perpetrators of these crimes are enemies of the human race. All of us who are hearing about what has happened for the first time need to listen. Ritual abuse and mind control is happening. This volume lets survivors and therapists speak for themselves.

References

Anon (2010). In the back: 20 years of satanic panic. *Private Eye*, 16 December.

Cassidy, S. (1977). *Audacity to Believe*. London: Collins.

Crews, F. (1990). *The Memory Wars*. New York: New York Review of Books.

DeMause, L. (1995). *The History of Childhood*. Northvale, NJ: Jason Aronson.

Fleck, L. (1979). *Genesis and Development of a Scientific Fact*. Chicago, IL: University of Chicago Press.

Grunbaum, A. (1985). *The Foundations of Psychoanalysis: A Philosophical Critique*. Berkeley CA: University of California Press.

Irving, D. (1986). Cited in Wikipedia, note 62.

MKULTRA document MORI ID 144686 (1952).

Schore, A. N. (1999). *Affect Regulation and the Origin of the Self: The Neurobiology of Emotional Development*. London: Psychology Press.

Schwartz, J. (1995a). Is physics really a good model for psychoanalysis? Reflections on Langs and Badalamenti. *British Journal of Psychotherapy*, 11: 595–601.

Schwartz, J. (1995b). What does the physicist know? Thraldom and insecurity in the relationship of psychoanalysis to physics. *Psychoanalytic Dialogues*, 5: 45–62.

Schwartz, J. (1996a). What is science? What is psychoanalysis? What is to be done? *British Journal of Psychotherapy*, 13: 53–63.

Schwartz, J. (1996b). Physics, philosophy, psychoanalysis and ideology. On engaging with Adolf Grunbaum. *Psychoanalytic Dialogues*, 6: 503–513.

Schwartz, J. (1999). *Cassandra's Daughter: A History of Psychoanalysis in Europe and America*. London: Penguin [reprinted London: Karnac, 2003].

Schwartz, J. (2000). Further adventures with Adolf Grunbaum. *Psychoanalytic Dialogues*, 10: 343–345.

CHAPTER ONE

What has changed in twenty years?

Valerie Sinason

T his subject is not easy. Indeed, this is a historic conference. It is an act of disobedience, of speaking out, of political, personal, and clinical ethics and advocacy. It comes from a crucial link between the Bowlby Centre, the Clinic for Dissociative Studies, and the Paracelsus Trust, which I started to aid clinic clients at the instigation of Pearl King, one of its benefactors. Now it is its own separate entity, which has the benefit of Pat Frankish as Chair, and Kate White, Orit Badouk Epstein, Deborah Briggs, Richard and Xenia Bowlby, Michael Curtis, and Brett Kahr as trustees. All agreed that this conference had an important educational aim.

It is the seminal work of John Bowlby and the relational approach to trauma that has offered the best way forward for many of us, together with a willingness to stand up and be counted. Indeed, just as John Bowlby recognized and acknowledged dissociative identity disorder (DID) and separation anxieties, his son, Sir Richard Bowlby, has continued to hold the torch, supporting unpopular and outcast areas of society and the mind.

Rachel Wingfield Schwartz and I were involved together with survivors who had been ritually abused over twenty years ago. It is also important that the Clinic for Dissociative Studies speaks up about this, as we have been very clear that the aetiology for DID that we witness in the consulting room comes largely, in our practice, from ritual organized crime.

For some people, some known and others invisible, coming to this conference has been an act of unbelievable heroism, of telling, of witnessing, of knowing. There will have been punishments for coming, for listening, for speaking. Some have not come, feeling that by staying away they have saved particular speakers and friends from being hurt. Others have come to stand between their protectors and the cult.

Last night, like many people here, I received e-mails and phone calls from different countries imploring me not to speak, as I would be killed. It was survivors who wrote, for whom the cruellest manipulation of attachment needs is exactly this: abusing someone's capacity for love and concern.

It is perhaps the cruellest lie and trick to make a child or vulnerable adult feel that expressing care for someone else could lead to his or her death.

Survivors in the audience have shown so clearly, and with great protection for us, the listeners, something of what they have gone through—the dilemmas and choices given to Trish and Ellen sharply showed the techniques of how this was done in the flower game. (There are many other programmes with flower games, too. No system in any survivor is identical.)

No wonder the so-called "easy" choices of the ordinary non-abuse world are so unbearable. What dress shall I buy? Which food shall I buy? Any choice is linked with danger and death. Everything comes from tests, and all tests are lethal.

So, what is different over twenty years? I will start with what is the same.

What has not changed in twenty years

The law: duress and ritual crime

I have the permission of a brave survivor, a professional called Lisa, to state this. Lisa went to the police to speak of all the crimes she had been forced to commit from earliest childhood to her late thirties, as well as all the crimes of which she had been the victim. The litany was familiar to all of us in this work (Hale & Sinason, 1994). Murder, fake murder, necrophilia, bestiality, abortion, cannibalism, oral, anal, and vaginal abuse, drinking blood, semen, and urine, eating faeces and non-food substances, drugs, pornography, and so on. If every survivor spoke out, then slowly the awareness might spread of what people were forced to do.

The Detective Inspector she bravely spoke to was very sympathetic and said the judge and jury would make some remission of sentence, he was sure, but as there was no plea bargaining in this country, and no law on duress, she could face a custodial sentence of some twelve years.

Until we join together to ask for a law on duress, many survivors will be left with an unbearable and unfair guilt their abusers have projected into them, aided and abetted by a non-understanding legal system.

Also, we have do not have ritual crime as a separate category of criminal offence. This means that accounts of spiders, snakes, masks, and unusual costumes do not count as evidence, unlike in Idaho, in the USA. Making children and adults eat non-food substances is also not a crime, so checking a stomach for insects, etc., would not be done.

Reality remains the problem

Outside of the "Adam" case (the poor Nigerian child whose mutilated body was found in the Thames), the subject is still not bearable. The "Adam" case was somehow bearable for racist reasons: he was a black child from "over there", not one of "ours". However, the use of white British middle-class and upper-class women, men, and children is still invisible.

The cruel treatment of the Baby Ps and Victoria Climbies who carry on living and do not obtain the peace of dying is just as intolerable to face as it ever was.

The pool of practitioners has not enlarged adequately. However, we have been a rather stable group, and thank heavens for Dr Joan Coleman, still working as hard as ever in her seventh decade. Joan Coleman provided me with a sanity check when I had my first British case over twenty years ago, and I will never forget entering her warm, containing RAINS meeting and knowing I could say what I had been told and would be believed.

Indeed, the experience mental health practitioners go through when describing this work to sceptical colleagues provides us with a shadow of what survivors feel.

Yes, there are more referrals, and more people are aware of ritual abuse, but we remain an amnesic alter-personality representing unwanted reality! While DID at least has a neuroscientific "cachet" to sweeten the pill of reality, attitudes to ritual abuse, especially within our particular British culture, do not change.

MPs, journalists, and police cannot take this much further, as they fear for their popularity. Here was the difference between a former British DCI, Chris Healey, at a past RAINS conference and Colonel Kobus Jonker, who, at that time, had formed the Occult Squad in South Africa. While DCI Chris Healey warned that British police were not prepared to hear this, and someone from the CID should be asked for, with the preface that this was a difficult subject, Kobus instantly put up slides of ritual mutilation and pointed to evidence and its meaning.

Obedience, hierarchy, and professionals fearing for their jobs

One client angrily commented, when I spoke of democracy *vs.* her cult loyalty, that nearly all the professionals she had met had just blindly obeyed their seniors whatever their true thoughts about appropriate treatment or action.

She was, of course, right. When faced with a senior practitioner who is sceptical, the most highly skilled people give up their brain!

So what is different?

In the late 1980s and early 1990s, almost everyone we saw said he or she was a survivor of Satanist abuse. Satanism, like Pagan and other belief systems, is totally legal now, and we have the first serving Satanist naval officers as well as Pagan police officers. Only a small number of members of any particular religion actively abuse. However, later referrals included Luciferians, those from Paganism, Wicca, Voodoo, Black Witchcraft, Black Dianetics,

Gnostic Luciferianism, Illuminati, Military Mind Control, MK Ultra, and Bluebird. Gradually, too, we saw victims of abuse within mainstream religions, abuse by mullahs, priests, vicars, and rabbis. Of even more concern were those whose systems can include all of this: a devoted Catholic alter, an abusing Satanist one, a Celtic one, a Kabbala one, an Egyptian one . . . None would want to know each other. The innate phobia between them is then enlarged by their opposing belief systems.

The change through a personal journey: publish and be saved

Without a new social paradigm, the change that happens is more the personal journey of the survivor and the therapist. There is evidence of the social change that has happened by the number of survivors present here today. And once survivors do all the talking and writing, we will truly have the paradigm shift that happened once the Women's Movement took on domestic abuse and child abuse.

It was, therefore, very good to hear from the Conference that ninety-year-old Betty's memoirs were shortly going to be published, and that Wanda Marriker's book, *Morning Come Quickly*, had appeared in the USA. Art therapist Ami Woods here works with a well-known artist, or, rather, group of artists in one body who happen to have DID, called Kim Noble, and we also have the cross-stitch work by Jane James.

So publish and be saved

Randy Noblitt, Pamela Perskin Noblitt (Noblitt & Perskin Noblitt, 2008), Ellen Lacter, Alison Miller, Jean Riseman, and Carole Rutz, all from the USA, help us.

In the meantime, the clinician's moral and personal journey is a crucial one. It took me a year to talk about ritual abuse, and when I handed the manuscript of *Treating Survivors of Satanist Abuse* to Edwina Welham at Routledge, I slept properly and no longer feared being killed, as I had done. I also felt enormous gratitude to my agent, Sara Menguc, for being willing to handle such a topic when she had hoped for me to write a book on family problems that affected everyone, based on my *Guardian* column!

If it took me a year to talk about ritual abuse because initially I felt silenced, it took me ten years to talk about mind control. It was thanks to colleagues Adah Sachs and Graeme Galton, who asked me to write about an incident that had haunted me for their book (Sachs & Galton, 2008), which led me through. I had been terrified of moving from ritual abuse to writing about mind control, but their gentle pressure released me. Ten years . . .

Art and creativity aid us all in this work, so I will end with a poem I wrote about it.

Treating Satanist abuse survivors

> In the garden a green breath rises and rises
> I am sitting by the window
> On the table your fax sends murder down the line
>
> In the hospital a woman asks for drugs
> A child is dying through her mouth
> Neither of them can speak
>
> In the morgue the dead child is calling for her mother
> As we write the scars on her head
> close like red zips
>
> In the wood dead dog hairs grow flesh
> Whimper, then howl for a kennel
>
> We put these things together
> Together we find a voice.

Appendix: Calendar abuse—the significance of ritual dates. Prepared for the Bowlby Centre and Clinic for Dissociative Studies Conference on Ritual Abuse, 23–24 September 2009 by Valerie Sinason with David Leevers

Introduction

"The fault, dear Brutus, lies in ourselves, not our stars"

(Shakespeare)

As our human species crossed the known continents, we took with us our awareness of day and night, light and dark, sky and earth,

sea, river, rain, floods, monsoons, mountains, thunder and lightning, wind. We took with us our awareness of other living crea-
tures, birds, fish, animals, and insects. Looking up at the skies, we
drew the constellations of stars and ascribed particular meanings to
sun and moon. Like frightened children trying to turn dots on a
night-time wall into a friendly shape, we have needed to ascribe
meaning and myth to planets and stars.

This is not to deny the possibility of many kinds of meanings
that are currently beyond our skills and comprehension, but to
point to the psychological need to defend against such huge
unknowns.

Faced with mortality, time, and the Cosmos, we needed belief
systems to sustain us; some were harsh, to mirror the social or
geographical environment, others offered hope and love. The
movement of peoples across the earth, dispersals and disposses-
sions, the growth of art and writing, led to an import and export of
deities. Winning a war truly did mean gods and goddesses were on
the side of the victors, and vanquished peoples took up the deities
of the victors.

History is the voice of the winner. However, the vanquished can
be heard in other ways. In the history of religious dates across the
world we can see the old vanquished gods and goddesses peeping
through the days that earlier were theirs but which were later trans-
posed to their victorious descendants. We cannot even be sure that
our earliest recorded history is the earliest. Where did the Sumerian
deities come from?

However, what is repressed can break through. For example, the
25th of December, ascribed to the birth of Jesus, is the birthday of
the Sun and, therefore, the most obvious date for Tammuz, the reincarnation of the Sun God. Tammuz was a Babylonian and Sumerian
god, and the tenth month of the Hebrew Calendar is named for
him.

Yule, the Winter Solstice on the 21st December, was moved by
the Roman Catholic Church to the 25th of December, which was
also the Roman Saturnalia festival, a time for drinking and feasting.
Druids at this period saw the mistletoe as representing sexuality,
and mistletoe, as with other ancient "props" was absorbed also. The
same processes, as you will see, affect other key dates in the
seasonal calendar.

The Edict of Milan

Although our multicultural British society means that we are meeting those who have been hurt through a variety of belief systems, the majority still have links with the Judeo-Christian heritage. Indeed, Christianity is currently still the world's largest religion. As a result of this, there is one major historical event that I consider crucial to consider.

For a belief system to gain a huge following it requires to be linked with a national identity. It was the conversion of Emperor Constantine of Rome that was to transform the chances of Christianity, which had previously been the religion of a persecuted minority. Constantine had declared that he would convert to the High God of Christianity if he won a particular battle, which he did. A year later he offered an edict that was remarkable in its tolerance. In 313 AD he announced "that it was proper that the Christians and all others should have liberty to follow that mode of religion which to each of them appeared best". He considered Rome would benefit from the prayers of all its different citizens and belief systems. No religion was illegal.

However, just a few years later, non-Christian belief systems lost their imperial support and funding, and the oppressor's former religion was now the victim, and finally designated the "pagan". Despite the current recognition of many of the belief systems that exist, the most ancient, that pre-date the major religions, have continued to be demonized or disavowed. Such rigid exclusion can be as damaging as complacent inclusion (witness the current religious trauma in Ireland) in making it easier for abusive practices to flourish.

Finally, ritual and ceremony are powerful processes and events that can enrich our lives and aid us at moments of greatest vulnerability or happiness: for example, births, deaths, and marriages. They are an intrinsic part of human existence and attachment. The focus of this text is concerned only with the tragedy that occurs where ritual and ceremony is used abusively.

How to use this

When children and adults made their brave way to speaking of abuse within religious or cult systems in the 1980s, they showed, through their verbal and non-verbal responses, that certain dates held enormous terror for them. Some, living with a supportive friend or partner, were able to disclose something about these dates. Many others had been taught for years, under the greatest threats of torture and punishment, to be silent. It soon emerged in treatment that they could face only too readily the threats to themselves. However, worst of all, their own loving capacity to attach was being abused. Those who terrified them were threatening to hurt anyone they disclosed to.

"Are you sure you are all right?" was the most common question asked of any therapist, counsellor, or friend after a disclosure.

After further years of work, survivors were able to let us know that there were some areas of terror where, if we named the unnameable, they would be free to express more. In a project on ritual abuse based at the Tavistock and Portman NHS Clinics in the early 1990s, Dr Robert Hale and myself found the majority of people who came to us were in particular states of terror on the 31st of October. By looking into the history and meanings of that date, we were able to provide some small easing of the pain being carried.

While the Internet is filled with details of all kinds of occult practices and all kinds of calendars, there is no substitute for a relationship in which a little trust might dare slowly to develop. Just as no two children in the same family have had exactly the same parents, no two children or adults hurt within any particular religion or cult experience it in exactly the same way.

To our amazement, some people can move forward without flashbacks into a new life of light and love, while others continue to be hurt anew with each ritual date. Some people carry post trauma responses to a few dates in the year, while for others, their whole life consists of being a slave to the calendar, with no respite, and with therapy as the only witness.

Where someone has been profoundly hurt in the context of a belief system, they can find all belief systems frightening and triggering and this calendar will carry a major health warning. For others, who have managed to have a secure attachment to a belief or a person, it can be of interest to see how key basic themes of human predicaments appear and reappear in different belief systems.

In other words, there is nothing prescriptive in this calendar. It is not a manual. It is not an exhaustive list of triggering times. Nothing can be a shortcut away from the painful shared task of bearing witness. However, I have a hope that it might help some understand why "calendar abuse" is one of the most lethal kinds of abuse (Sinason, 1994).

When I began working with survivors of ritual abuse, I found that their abuse was often linked to the Christian concept of Satan. Since then I and other therapists at the Clinic for Dissociative Studies, the Bowlby Centre, and elsewhere, have worked with survivors of abuse within the world's greatest mainstream religions, let alone sects and cults. Unerringly, we found that men and women from all over the UK, who did not know each other, were all falling ill, or being attacked, or suffering flashbacks on the same dates.

They show us, yet again, how our human hopes to understand the great unknown are beset with all the cruelties and unworked-through trauma of our species as well as the hope for something better.

Survivors of ritual abuse of any kind come from all social classes, all religious backgrounds, all racial groups, all ages, and all levels of education. While dissociative defences can allow some to continue with an apparently normal life with their pain invisible except to those who know them, others are profoundly visible, with the toll of flashbacks and problems with regulation of mood.

While there are survivors who come forward and write accounts of what has happened in their life in order to help others, many of these are, understandably, anonymous. There are also survivor-professionals who write from their professional context and need the freedom to not have to disclose their lived experience. While the climate continues to be unsafe, although more understanding than twenty years ago, there is more impetus for therapists and others to speak the unwanted message to the rest of society.

This is especially true when the subject is about belief. Speaking about hurt within a religious context can evoke fears of being seen as illiberal and intolerant. There is also the deep fear of threats coming from fundamentalists of all belief systems, let alone members of groups who hurt others.

I consider it helpful to make clear that I am not talking about any religion *per se*, only the human representation of it. I am particularly talking about attachment patterns. Those with a secure attachment to their religion (as to their family, nationality, place of work) are able to speak confidently about the positives and negatives of their experiences. It is those with a disorganized attachment who will fight to the death for the honour of a maltreating parent, deity, or religious representatives. As one wise religious leader told me, "It is a sin of pride to think you have to fight for God's honour—you are implying He does not have the power to stand up for Himself."

Towards a definition of spiritual abuse

Spiritual abuse is the enforcement of a position of power, leadership or attachment in which total unquestioning obedience in thought, word or action is demanded of a child, adolescent or adult under threat of punishment in this life and in an afterlife for themselves, their families, helpers or others.

In this abuse, there is no room for the individual to be allowed their own relationship with the divine as the abusers claim they are the only link. [Sinason & Aduale, "Safeguarding London's Children" Conference, June 2008]

Towards a definition of ritual abuse

A significant amount of all abuse involves ritualistic behaviour, such as a specific date, time, position and repeated sequence of actions. Ritual Abuse, however, is the involvement of children, who cannot give consent, in physical, psychological, emotional, sexual and spiritual abuse which claim to relate the abuse to beliefs and settings of a religious, magical or supernatural kind. Total unquestioning obedience in thought, word or action is demanded of such a child, adolescent or adult under threat of punishment in this life and in an afterlife for themselves, their families, helpers or others. [Sinason & Aduale, "Safeguarding London's Children" Conference, 2008]

Ritual as defence against fear of mortality

"Who turns and stands there lingering—
that's how we live always
saying goodbye"
[Rainer Maria Rilke, 8th elegy, p. 153]

Freud considered that there were four unbearable factors for our species:

- we are not the masters of the universe,
- we are descended from apes,
- we are not masters of our unconscious,
- and we are not immortal.

Copernicus and Galileo discovered that the earth was not the centre of the universe. This rocked the Western Church. Our second most impossible subject is that of our own ancestry. We descend from other animals. Our longing to see our births and lives as having special meaning over and beyond that of other living beings can stir up the need to invest extra significance in our position among other animals and other species. This may not have been such a problem to pre-Judeo-Christian culture, where there were animal, bird, and location Gods.

A third wound is that we are not masters of our unconscious and can be taken unawares in all kinds of ways by our own internal processes.

The fourth, and perhaps most important, difficulty lies in coming to terms with our own mortality. Time, mortality, and the cosmos are key areas that both thrill and terrify us. Religions and other belief systems try to offer us ways of making sense of the meaning of our existence and our place in the universe.

Where there is secure attachment, towards family, friends, or belief system, there is a greater capacity to be protected from the persuasion of abusive religions and cults and to benefit and be enriched by loving ones. Where there is insecure attachment, or, especially, a disorganized attachment, there is greater need or vulnerability to shape a universe where everything is accounted for and ordered as either the master or as the slave.

In trying to make sense of changes of seasons, day turning into night, thunder and lightning, volcanoes, tidal waves, the position of the planets, the nightly death of the sun and monthly coming of the moon, it is not surprising that almost every belief system struggles to find a reason for birth and death, sacrifice and hope, and that the meaning of "sacrifice" becomes literal, not just symbolic. Fear of sexuality, body fluids, what comes out of a woman's body, a wish to control procreation and primitive responses to the newborn baby become transformed into rules and punishments. Attachment needs are denied by turning them into rigid and hurtful rituals, rather than transforming creative ones. Guilt about surviving when others die leads to the need for more blood sacrifice, which slowly, in safer countries, transforms into symbolic sacrifice.

It is not, therefore, surprising that responses to particular dates can be frightening to survivors of abuse by mainstream, minor, and fringe religions, as well as to survivors of cult abuse, which are often the abusive leftovers from earlier primitive mainstream religions.

Sadly, beyond all this, we know through Milgram's obedience experiments that even the more securely attached individuals, when faced with the group power of unreason and cruelty, give in to living and behaving in a barbarous way.

Time and calendars and repetition compulsion

September, the time for starting school in the UK and the northern hemisphere. Autumn days. Many adults can remember on such days the excitement of a new pencil-case, exercise books, covering a text book, excitement as well as anxiety at starting school. Others who were bullied and terrorized in school remember the season with dread. Our memories are evoked by dates and seasons. Sometimes "calendar abuse" hurts more than other abuse because just a time or day of the week can trigger flashbacks and horrific memories without another human being even needing to be there.

From earliest human experience, the seasons have made a huge impact on our psyches as well as night and day, sun, moon, stars, wind, rain, thunder, and lightning. To deal with the impossibility of time, all human cultures have needed to create a calendar that links our species with deities. Where there is a deity standing for love, these dates can bring joy and celebration. Where the deities are gods or goddesses of punishment or hatred, the dates can bring pain and terror. Sometimes a date can be a mixture. Most belief systems include ideas of the death of a god and rebirth, sky gods and underground gods, twins and murder/sacrifice linked to the seasons, the stars and planets, and the sun and moon, the transience of the individual *vs.* the permanence of the heavens.

Our established religions, in their early days, were highly intelligent in trying to woo public interest by keeping alive seasonal dates already linked to older religions but giving them another name! So, looking into the meaning of dates that can be triggering provides a multicultural theological and historical lesson in cultural archaeology.

It is very hard to consider that a date that has precious meaning, whether spiritually or emotionally, to one individual, can mean such abject terror for another. We need to try to preserve our own pleasure in certain dates while understanding the pain they can cause others.

In addition to the key universal yearly dates, such as the new moons, full moons, solstices, equinoxes, etc., different cults and religious groups also have other dates that are special. Personal birthdays, family birthdays, deaths, and wedding anniversaries are included. Even the clinician's, partner's, or friend's birthday are significant. Should a personal date fall on a ritual/religious date, there is even greater impact. Should a personal or religious date fall at a weekend then there is even more time dedicated to it.

Many belief systems also have an attraction to numerology—the magic meaning of numbers. Humans have found different ways of counting to try to control time and the uncertainty of life and have ascribed different religious and mystical values to the existence of certain numbers. This means that, in addition to key festival times, other dates have particular numerical meaning, including the survivor's age on their birthday. There are 650,000 references to numerology on the Internet, and interest in birth signs and horoscopes is part of this.

Numbers are also linked to different ages of development which have religious meaning in different belief systems: for example, baptism, barmitzvah, marriage to Christ or Satan.

A birthday that also falls on an occult date (which is planned in some generational families by inducing birth) therefore has a double meaning, and if it also falls on a Friday, Saturday, or Sunday in a given year it has even greater impact.

Calendars, years, and months

The current occult calendar consists of four periods of thirteen weeks each. Thirteen is the number that signifies rebellion in the Judeo-Christian tradition as there were thirteen at the Last Supper. We can now see why Friday the 13th is seen as so doubly unlucky. Should Friday 13th also be a full moon or another occult date, it triggers even more fear. The superstition around the number thirteen goes back farther. In Norse mythology there were thirteen present at a banquet in Valhalla when Balder (son of Odin) was slain, which led to the downfall of the gods. Friday the 13th will happen between one and three times in any given year.

Twenty-eight was a special number linked to the menstrual cycle. Alistair Crowley saw twenty-eight as the number of the Beast, Bahimiron. Twenty-eight also means power for Cabbalists. Numbers divisible by three also are given extra meaning—with Revelations saying 666 is the name of the Beast.

The Kabbalah has a whole system of meanings linked to numbers.

Numbers have also been necessary to control the way the movement of our planet is measured.

The Maya tracked a fault in the solar year in which they counted 365 days per year. Because they could not use fractions, the "quarter" day left over every year caused their calendar to drift with regard to the actual solar year. The 365-day year contained months that were also given names.

The Sumerian Calendar, sixth century BC noted Mercury, Venus, Mars, Jupiter, and Saturn, as well as sun and moon, and synchronized a lunar calendar of twelve lunar months a year with an extra month inserted every four years. The early Egyptians and Greeks copied this.

The Babylonian Calendar and the *Jewish Calendar* followed a lunar month (Genesis 1:14) and special offerings were given on the day of the new moon.

The Islamic Calendar, the lunar calendar used by Muslims, dates from 622 AD (the year of the Hegira); the beginning of the Muslim year retrogresses through the solar year, completing the cycle every thirty-two years. The Islamic (Muslim) year begins with Muharram. All Islamic dates are subject to sighting of the moon; an event that may be one day earlier or later than the date listed.

The Celtic Year was a solar year, marked by four major bonfire feasts a year dedicated to the sun.

Hindu Calendar. The year is divided into twelve lunar months, but, because of the shortfall, it becomes lunisolar. The solar year is divided into twelve lunar months in accordance with the successive entrances of the sun into the signs of the zodiac, the months varying in length from twenty-nine to thirty-two days.

Jewish Calendar (Judaism): the calendar used by Jews dates from 3761 BC (the assumed date of the creation of the world); a lunar year of 354 days is adjusted to the solar year by periodic leap years.

Gregorian Calendar: the solar calendar now in general use in the UK and used by Christians in the West was introduced by Gregory XIII in 1582 to correct an error in the Julian calendar by suppressing ten days, making 5 October be called 15 October, and providing that only centenary years divisible by 400 should be leap years; it was adopted by Great Britain and the American colonies in 1752.

Buddhist Calendar. Apart from the Japanese, most Buddhists use the Lunar calendar. The most significant celebration happens every May on the night of the full moon, when Buddhist all over the world celebrate the birth, enlightenment, and death of the Buddha over 2500 years ago. It has become known as Buddha Day.

Pagan Calendar. By the third century the term Pagan, or "Paganus", was used to mean all those who were not Christians. Slowly, it took on a more disparate meaning and the term is now often seen as an umbrella term that covers many belief systems such as Druids (who have their own calendar), followers of Asatru, who adhere to the ancient, pre-Christian Norse religion, Wiccans, who follow pre-Celtic beliefs, and those who follow the religions of ancient Rome, Greece, or Egypt.

Contemporary Satanism, as espoused by Anton La Vey, was created on 1st May 1966 through the San Fransisco Church of Satan. As with many religious leaders, he chose an auspicious date on which to launch his church. He has considered that the highest holiday in Satanism is the date of one's own birthday, in direct contrast to religions that deify "an anthropomorphic form of their own image" instead of seeing themselves as a god, as in Christianity (Ecclesiastes 7:1) where " the day of death [is better] than the day of one's birth". Satanism is a legal belief system in the UK.

Shintoism, Jainism, Bahai, Luciferianism, Chinese traditional religion, African religions, and all the branches of Christianity all have dates in common.

Christianity is the largest world religion (including all its sub-sects and branches) and Scientology is the smallest among the religions that are counted in national statistics.

Ceremonial time

When does a ceremony begin? According to the Eastern Orthodox Church calendar, the day begins after evening vespers at sunset and concludes with vespers on the following day. For this reason, the observance of all Eastern Orthodox holy days and Jewish holy days begins at sunset on the evening before the holy day.

Do not assume that because someone has been triggered by one date that they will be by all the ritual dates, as each abusing group behaves differently and prioritizes different dates. Only the survivor knows at what time the bad dates are most relevant and which dates these are.

Days of the week

For some survivors, a day has significance only if a ceremony happens to fall on it. For others, days of the week have a mystical meaning regardless of the week or month it is linked to. We can be so used to measuring our time in days and months that we lose sight of the fact that the names provide understanding of deep meanings.

Sunday is the first day of the week. From prehistoric times to the close of the fifth century of the Christian era, the worship of the sun was dominant. Sunday celebrates the sun god, Ra, Helios, Apollo, Ogmios, Mithrias, the sun goddess, Phoebe. In the year 321, Constantine the Great ruled that the first day of the week, "the venerable day of the sun", should be a day of rest. The Christian concept of resting on the Sunday was borrowed.

Monday is the day of the moon goddess.

Tuesday is the third day of the week. Tiw's day is derived from Tyr of Tir, the God of honourable war, the wrestler and the son of Odin, the Norse god of war, and Frigga, the earth mother.

Wednesday comes from the Scandinavian Woden (Odin), chief god of Norse mythology, who was often called the All Father and is linked to the Roman Dies Mercurii.

Thursday comes from Thor, the God of strength and thunder, who is the counterpart of Jupiter, or Jove. Thor is the only god who cannot cross from earth to heaven upon the rainbow, for he is so heavy and powerful that the gods fear it will break under his weight. It was said that whenever Thor threw his hammer, the noise of thunder was heard through the heavens.

Friday is derived from the Germanic Frigga, the name of the Norse God Odin's wife. Frigga is considered to be the mother of all, and the goddess who presides over marriage. The name means loving or beloved. The corresponding Latin name is Dies Veneris, a day dedicated to Venus, the goddess of love. Any Friday that falls on the thirteenth day of the month has a ritual meaning. Friday is the unluckiest day of the week for many Christians, who believe that Christ was crucified on this day.

Saturday is corresponding to the Roman Dies Saturni, or day of Saturn, the Roman god of agriculture. Saturday is also represented by Loki, the Norse god of tricks and chaos. Saturn is also linked to the Greek God Cronus, who devoured his children.

For Jews, the Sabbath and day of rest is Saturday.

It is worth noting the similarity of the names of days with Sun Day, Moon Day, Mars Day, Mercury Day, Jupiter's Day, Venus's Day, Saturn's Day.

Months

January comes from Janus, the two-headed God of doorways: the month was named by Pompilus, the second king of Rome ca 700 BC.

February is the Roman festival of purification that was held on the 15th of that month.

March/Martius was the original beginning of the year and the time for the resumption of war. Mars is the Roman god of war. He is identified with the Greek god Ares.

April comes from Aphrodite, the Greek goddess of love and beauty. She is identified with the Roman goddess Venus. Called Aprilis, from aperire, "to open", possibly because it is the month in which the buds begin to open.

May is derived from Maia (meaning "the great one"), the Italian goddess of spring, the daughter of Faunus, and wife of Vulcan.

June comes from Juno, the principle goddess of the Roman Pantheon. She is the goddess of marriage and the well-being of women. She is the wife and sister of Jupiter. She is identified with the Greek goddess Hera. However, the name might also come from *iuniores* (young men, juniors) as opposed to maiores (grown men, majors) for May, the two months being dedicated to young and old men.

July: Julius Caesar reformed the Roman calendar (hence, the Julian calendar) in 46 BC. In the process, he renamed this month after himself.

August. Augustus Caesar clarified and completed the calendar reform of Julius Caesar. In the process, he also renamed this month after himself.

September, Latin for the seventh month, had thirty days until Numa, when it had twenty-nine days, until Julius, when it reverted to being thirty days long.

October, meaning eighth month, has always had thirty-one days.

Novembris, meaning ninth month, had thirty days until Numa, when it had twenty-nine days, until Julius, when it reverted to being thirty days long.

December had thirty days until Numa, when it had twenty-nine days, until Julius, when it became thirty-one days long

Numa Pompilius, the second king of Rome ca 700 BC, added the two months Januarius and Februarius. He also changed the number of days in several months to be odd, a lucky number. After Februarius, there was occasionally an additional month of *Intercalaris* "intercalendar". This is the origin of the leap-year day being in February. In 46 BC, Julius Caesar reformed the Roman calendar (hence, the Julian calendar) changing the number of days in many months and removing *Intercalaris*.

Dates that change: Easter and moons

While most ritual dates stay the same, dates based on the lunar calendar change each year and therefore need special attention.

Ash Wednesday, Easter

The dates of Easter weekend, Easter Sunday, Good Friday, Ash Wednesday, Ascension, Pentecost, Corpus Christi, first Sunday of Advent, Full Moons, and New Moons all change.

No new moons or full moons are shown in the monthly calendar provided, as they vary.

All phases of the moon have meaning, from new moon, first quarter, waxing gibbous, full moon, waning gibbous, last quarter.

The second new moon is called the Black Moon. Blue Moon is the second full moon to occur in a single calendar month. Two new moons and two full moons in one calendar month is seen to have more power.

The interval between full moons is about 29.5 days, while the average length of a month is 30.5 days. This makes it very unlikely that any given month will contain two full moons.

Eclipses also have meaning.

The quarter moon represents the moon goddess Diana, and Lucifer, the morning star. If we consider that the planet named Venus is sometimes called the morning star and sometimes the evening star and that the same name was given to Lucifer, we can see the way the emblems of different belief systems join together.

Table 1 shows some of the names given to the moon according to the month.

The seasons and weather

It is worth noting that while Western world beliefs have four seasons, there are other cultures that have or have had three seasons. For example, in Ancient Egypt, there was Akhet, the inundation (June–September), Peret (October–February), the Growing Season, and Shemu (March–May), the Harvesting Season.

Thunder, lightning, storm winds, and rain all have different meaning and different deities attached to them.

Table 1.   Names of the moon according to month.

January	Old Moon	Wolf Moon	Moon after Yule, Ice Moon
February	Wolf Moon	Snow Moon	Hunger Moon, Storm Moon, Candles Moon
March	Lenten Moon	Worm Moon	Crow Moon, Crust Moon, Sugar Moon, Sap Moon, Chaste Moon
April	Egg Moon	Pink Moon	Sprouting Grass Moon, Fish Moon, Seed Moon, Waking Moon
May	Milk Moon	Flower Moon	Corn Planting Moon, Corn Moon, Hare's Moon
June	Flower Moon	Strawberry Moon	Honey Moon, Rose Moon, Hot Moon, Planting Moon
July	Hay Moon	Buck Moon	Thunder Moon, Mead Moon
August	Grain Moon	Sturgeon Moon	Red Moon, Green Corn Moon, Lightning Moon, Dog Moon
September	Corn Moon	Harvest Moon	Corn Moon, Barley Moon
October	Harvest Moon	Hunter's Moon	Travel Moon, Dying Grass Moon, Blood Moon
November	Hunter's Moon	Beaver Moon	Frost Moon, Snow Moon
December	Oak Moon	Cold Moon	Frost Moon, Long Night's Moon, Moon Before Yule

The significant dates per month

January

1:      New Year's Day. A Druid (spirit) feast day (light fires on hill tops).

5:      Shivaratri (night of Shiva creator/destroyer).

5 or 6: Twelfth Night.

6:      Dionysian revels.

6:      Kore gives birth/manifestation of divinity. Kore, Demeter, and Persephone make up the triple goddess.

6:      Epiphany. This refers to celebration over the manifestation of the divinity of Jesus, as shown by the visit of the three Magi.

7:      Eastern Orthodox Christmas.

7:      St Winebald Day. Winebald was a successful Saxon missionary who founded the Benedictine Order and was the brother and son of saints.

12:     Birth of both Rosenburg and Goering, Nazi leaders in the Second World War.

13:     Satanic New Year.

15–16: Skillfest, the feast day of St Henry of Coquet Island, a Dane who settled here in the twelfth century, noted for his psychic perceptions.

17:     Feast of Fools (Old Twelfth Night)/satanic and demon revels.

18:     Old Epiphany.

18–22: Dream Festival (Pleiades).

20:     St Agnes' Eve.

20–27: Grand climax (blood rituals). St Agnes, the patron saint of virgins, was martyred at the age of twelve or thirteen for being a Christian. On this day in Rome, the Pope blesses two lambs. Young virgins can have visions of delight on such a night. In the Satanic calendar, it is the conjuration of Telal, a warrior demon

30:     Hitler named Chancellor of Germany

February

1–3:   Mysteries of Persephone, Groundhog Day, Groundhog's Day. The popular "Punxsutawney Phil" groundhog comes out of his burrow to divine the next few weeks of weather. If he sees his shadow, there is a prediction that there will be six more weeks of bad weather until Spring finally arrives; if he does not see his shadow, the next seven weeks before Spring will be good weather. This pagan tradition features both the numbers "6" and "7", which, when added, equals "13". Groundhog's Day (Imbolg) represents the Earth Mother in some systems. As the Earth goddess sleeps inside the earth during the winter season, so does the groundhog. They represent rebirth and renewal.

The name "groundhog" was substituted for the Satanic name of the holiday, Imbolg, a night requiring human sacrifice.

2: Candlemas (Imbolc/Imbolg). This date is halfway between winter and spring solstices and means "with milk" for both goats and cows. Brigid's Day (2 February) was the Christianized version of Brigid or Bride, the great Celtic Mother goddess. The Irish called it Imbolc, and it celebrates the triple goddess. It is also called Candlemas, as candles are blessed on that day.

9: (Starts evening of 8 February.) Tu B'Shevat (Jewish celebration of spring).

13: Friday the 13th.

14: Valentine's Day is a pagan festival that encourages love and physical lust. It is celebrated precisely thirteen days after Imbolg, thus imprinting upon it the number "13", Satan's number of extreme rebellion. Most people view this day now as the day to honour your wife or lover.

Cupid, the son of Venus, is really Tammuz, son of Semiramis. Venus, daughter of Jupiter, is really Semiramis herself.

Jupiter is the head deity, a sun god. Nimrod, Semiramis's husband, is considered a sun god in the Babylonian Mysteries.

The name of this month comes from the Roman goddess Februa and St Febronia (from Febris, the fever of love). She is the patroness of the passion of love. Her orgiastic rites are celebrated on 14 February—still observed as St Valentine's Day—when, in Roman times, young men would draw billets naming their female partners. This is a time of clear vision into other worlds, expressed by festivals of purification.

St Valentine was not mentioned until 496 AD and there is still doubt about his origins.

14: Fertility rituals.

15: Lupercalia (she-wolf mother of Romulus and Remus: honouring of Pan).

16: Presidents' Day (a federal holiday in the USA).

21–22: Feralia/Terminalia (Roman All Souls'/boundary day).

25: Walpurgis. Saint Walpurga herself was a niece of Saint Boniface and said to be a daughter of the Saxon prince, Saint Richard. Together with her brothers she travelled to Germany, where she became a nun. Her feast day is commemorated on 1st May.

March

28:    Hearthday, the day of Vesta, the matriarchal Roman goddess, who kept a perpetual fire on hearth and altar.

Easter varies each year between March and April. It is celebrated on the first Sunday after the first new moon after Ostara.
This date celebrates the return of Semiramis into her reincarnated
form of the Spring Goddess. The equivalent of Good Friday, "Easter
Friday", has historically been timed to be the third full moon from
the start of the year. Since the marrying of pagan Easter to Jesus'
resurrection, Good Friday is permanently fixed on the Friday prior
to Easter.

Within some abusive branches of Satanism and Luciferianism,
some children aged 3–5 are reborn through a cow corpse, or sometimes goats. There are also mock crucifixions.

Easter is steeped in the Babylonian Mysteries, The Babylonian
goddess, Ishtar, is the one for whom Easter is named. She was
Semiramis, wife of Nimrod, and the real founder of the Babylonian
Mysteries. After Nimrod died, Semiramis created the legend that he
was really her divine son born to her in a virgin birth. She is considered to be the co-founder of all occult religions, along with Nimrod.
Babylon: Ishtar (Easter), also called the Moon Goddess.

Catholics: Virgin Mary (Queen of Heaven) She links with the
Indian Indrana, the ancient Jewish Ashtoreth, the Sumerian
Innanna, the Greek Aphrodite and Ceres, the Egyptian Isis, and the
Etruscan Nutria.

The Babylonians celebrated the day as the return of Ishtar
(Easter), the goddess of Spring. This day celebrated the rebirth, or
reincarnation, of Nature and the goddess of Nature. According to
Babylonian legend, a huge egg fell from heaven, landing in the
Euphrates River. The goddess Ishtar (Easter) broke out of this egg.
Later, the feature of an egg nesting was introduced, a nest where the
egg could incubate until hatched. A "wicker" or reed basket was
conceived in which to place the Ishtar egg.

The Easter Egg Hunt was conceived because, if anyone found
her egg while she was being "reborn", she would bestow a blessing
upon that lucky person. Because this was a joyous Spring festival,
eggs were coloured with bright Spring colours.

The goddess's totem, the Moon-hare, would lay eggs for good children to eat. Eostre's hare was the shape that Celts imagined on the surface of the full moon Thus, "Easter"—Eostre, or Ishtar—was a goddess of fertility. Since the rabbit is a creature that procreates quickly, it symbolized the sexual act; the egg symbolized "birth" and "renewal". Together, the Easter Bunny and the Easter Egg symbolize the sex act and its offspring, Semiramis and Tammuz.

Easter offerings are derived from the tradition where the priests and priestesses would bring offerings to the temples for Easter. They brought freshly cut spring flowers and sweets to place on the altar of the god they worshipped. They would also bake hot cross buns, decorating them with crosses symbolizing the cross of Wotan, or another god. The first instance of hot cross buns can be traced back to about 1,500 BC, to Cecrops, the founder of Athens. In Old Testament celebrations in Israel, women angered God because they baked this type of cakes to offer them in worship to the Queen of Heaven (Jeremiah 17:17–18).

Another popular Easter offering was freshly made or purchased clothes. The priests would wear their best clothes, while the Vestal Virgins would wear newly made white dresses. They would also wear headgear, like bonnets, while many would adorn themselves in garlands of spring flowers. They would carry wicker baskets filled with foods and candies to offer to the gods and goddesses.

Easter sunrise services were originated by the priest serving the Babylonian Ishtar to symbolically hasten the reincarnation of Ishtar/Easter.

Lent has been accepted by the Roman Catholic Church. However, it is a commemoration of Tammuz's death. He was killed by a wild boar when he was forty years old. Lent was commemorated for exactly forty days prior to the celebration of Ishtar/Esotre and other goddesses.

March

1: St Eichstadt. Conjuring of Ninkharsag, Queen of Demons, and Ninkaszi, Horned Queen of Demons, drinking of blood.
2: Dionysian revels.
9: Festival of Ishtar (Astarte, Aphrodite, Venus).

10:     (Starts evening of 9th.) Purim.

15:     Ides of March: rites of Cybele and Attis (begins twelve day death and resurrection ritual). Cybele was a Phyrigian mother goddess who fell in love with the mortal, Attis. In her jealousy, when he fell in love with another mortal, she drove him mad so that he castrated and killed himself. Zeus helped her to resurrect him.

16:     Montsegur Day. In remembrance of the persecution of the Cathars.

17:     St Patrick's Day.

18:     Sheila-na-gig (Sheelah's Day, Sheelahis Day, Celtic creatress): Jacques De Molay Day (Knights Templar).

20–22: Pelusia, invocation of Isis (Hindi), Holi/Tubulustrum Roman purification/Shab-i-barat. Night of Forgiveness (Islam), Homage to the God of death.

21:     Spring Equinox. Children dedicated to Satan or Tiamet.

21–22: Goddess Ostara (Ishtar, also spelled, Eostre), for whom "Easter" is named. Easter is the first Sunday after the first new moon after Ostara.
        Eostre is mentioned in Beowulf, possibly identified with Kali. Red Easter eggs are placed on graves in Russia to assist rebirth.

21–24: Feast of the Beast/Bride of Satan/Feast of Priapus/Festival of Isis).

31–1 April: Vertmass, feast of green, linked with Green George, the goddess's consort who was the Green King of the woodland, or the fool of love.

April

1:      April Fools Day: precisely thirteen weeks since New Year's Day.

6:      Palm Sunday.

8:      Day of the Masters.

9:      Maundy Thursday. This commemorates the Last Supper of Jesus with the Apostles and falls on the Thursday before Easter.

12:     Hitler's birthday (alternate).

19:     This is the first day of the thirteen-day Satanic ritual relating to fire, the fire god, Baal, or Molech/Nimrod (the Sun

God), also known as the Roman god, Saturn (Satan/Devil). This day is a major human sacrifice day, demanding fire sacrifice with an emphasis on children. This day is one of the most important sacrifice days in Satanist abuse groups.

19: Anniversary of the day in 1943 when, after trapping the last Jewish resistance fighters in Warsaw in a storm drain and holding them there for several days, Nazi storm troopers began to pour fire into each end of the drain, using flame-throwers. They continued pouring the fire into the drain until all fighters were dead.

20: Hitler's birthday.

20: Queen's Day (Netherlands).

21–1: May: Grand Climax/Da Meur/preparation for Beltane.

22–29: Preparation for sacrifice in some abusive Satanic sects (third week of April).

23: St George's Day/England's national day.

26–1 May: Corpus de Baahl

30: Walpurgisnacht (May Eve). This is the day before May Day, when, in German occult tradition, a major festival takes place. Very cleverly, Christianity took over the date and named it Walpurgisnacht after a Christian Nun, Walburga, who was born in the UK in the eighth century but ran an enlightened nunnery in Germany. She had two religious brothers, St Willibald and St Winebald, who had set up the monasteries there. Her remains were transferred to Eichstatt on May Day, which is how St Eichadat's Day, May Day, and Beltane became linked.

30: Anniversary of Hitler's death. This tradition was strong enough that Adolf Hitler decided to kill himself on April 30 at 3:30p.m., thus creating a "333" and placing his suicide sacrifice within the Beltane time frame.

30–5 May: Grand Climax/Da Meur/Beltane

May

1: May Day. Beltane Fire Festival. Major Celtic festival.
This is the Greatest Sabbat, and is marked by fertility rites in open fields. Seminal fluid is mixed with dirt and insects and inserted into the vagina of a virgin. If conception occurs, the children are children

of Tiamet and Dur (Indur). Great bonfires are lit on the Eve of Beltane, 30 April, in order to welcome the Earth goddess. Participants hope to gain favour with this goddess so she will bless their families with procreative fertility. Since fertility is being asked of the Earth goddess, the Maypole is the phallic symbol and the circular dance around the pole forms the circle that is symbolic of the female sex organ. Four six-foot alternating red and white ribbons were connected to the pole; the men would dance counterclockwise, while the ladies danced clockwise. The union of the intertwining red and white ribbons symbolized the act of copulation.

For the Celts it marked the beginning of summer and the need to protect cattle from disease. For some, the great bonfires in Ireland were to protect cattle from witchcraft. In the past, this date was also dedicated to Mari, Mother Sea, as late as 1678 in Ireland.

9–13:   Lumeria (three days Roman All Souls).
11:      Mother's Day.
21–24: Rituals to mock the Ascension of Jesus to heaven, Ascension Day.
29–5 June: (Starts evening of 28 May.) Shavuot.
29–30: Memory Day dedicated to Joan of Arc.
31:      Pentecost (Whitsunday).

June

1:      Republic Day (Ireland)
3:      Eastern Orthodox Ascension Day
6:      D-Day (allied troops' invasion of France in the Second World War).
21:     Summer Solstice. Can be marked by torture, rape, and sacrifice of traitors, sacrifice and consumption of an infant.
21:     Father's Day.
23:     Midsummer's Eve / St John's Eve Fire Festival.
24:     Lighting the midwinter bonfires in New Zealand.

July

1:      Satanic and demon revels. Blood sacrifice.
4:      Independence Day in the USA.

14:      Bastille Day in France.
17–23:   Sacrifice of first-born males, communion given with their flesh and blood.
19–20:   Sunfest. The title and meaning of Helios was later given to St Elias.
23:      Beginning of Dog Days, linked to Sirius, the Dog Star, Sothis, star of Set.
25:      St James' Day / Festival of the horned god.
26:      Parents' Day.
30:      (Starts evening of 29th.) N Tish B'Av.

August

1:       Lammas / Lughnasadh (31st July, too). Lammas may be a corruption of "loaf mass", the celebration of the corn harvest. Lammas is midway between the summer solstice and the autumnal equinox. The wheel of the year is seen to shift from growing time to harvest time.
3:       Satanic and demon revels.
12–13:   Diana's day: the Roman name for the triple goddess, goddess of the moon and the three moon phases. Christians turned it into the Assumption of the Virgin Mary.
15:      Assumption of the Blessed Virgin Mary.
24:      Mania (opening of nether world gate).
24–27:   Fundus Mundi (a three day late-harvest festival).
26:      Preparation for Feast of the Beast, or marriage to Satan. Fasting and anointing.
28:      Feast of Nephthys (wife of Set, goddess of death).

September

1:       Labour Day
5–7:   Marriage to the Beast (Satan)
7:       Feast of the Beast, marriage of virgins to Satan.
13:      Grandparents' Day
19–20:   (Starts evening of 18th.) Rosh Hashanah.
20–21:   Midnight Host, vows and hierarchy fasting for previous week. Personal blood sacrifice from tip of fingers / paw of pet, etc., hands planted in the ground for power.

21:    Autumn/Fall Equinox, Mahon. From this date through Halloween, occultists believe the veil separating the earthly dimension from the demonic realm gets progressively thinner, with the thinnest night being 31 October; this thinning of the separating veil makes it easier for the demonic realm to enter the earthly dimension. Thus, on Halloween, evil spirits, ghosts, witches, hobgoblins, black cats, fairies, and demons of all sorts were believed to be running amok across the land. They had to be back in their spiritual dimension before midnight, Halloween, for the separating veil would then get thicker.

Jewish New Year period of Purification, Rosh Hashanah (date varies) and Yom Kippur (date varies), Day of Atonement.

23–30:   Birthday celebration of Shri Krishna.
23:    Mysteries of Eleusis.
28:    (Starts evening of 27th) Yom Kippur.
29:    Michaelmas.

October

2:    Last day of Mysteries of Eleusis.
2:    Durga Puja (Kali).
3–11:   (Starts evening of 2nd.) Sukkot, Shmini Atzeret/Simchat Torah.
5:    Opening of Mundus Cereris.
10:    Dashara (Kali's victory over Mahishasura).
12:    Dia de la Raza (Mexico).
12/20:   Hitler's half birthday.
13:    Backwards date re Halloween;13 as reverse of 31.
16:    Death of Rosenburg.
17–18:   Yom Kippur.
19:    Death of Goering.
20/23:   Hitler's half birthday.
22–29:   Preparation for All Hallows' Eve.
31:    Halloween/Samhain/All Hallows Eve/ Hallowmas/All Souls' Day, Halloween.

Preparation for the Isia (ring of six: Isis, Hathor, Nepthys, Horus, Thoth, Anubis). Resurrection of Osiris.

Start of the Celtic new year, the "dark" half of the year.

All Hallows Eve, as designated by the Catholic Church. This date is the Illuminati's highest day. Historically, Halloween is the deadliest ceremony dedicated to the Celtic Lord of the Dead, also symbolized by the horned god and the stag god. The Druids celebrated Samhain as a three-day fire festival, building huge bonfires, thought to ward off demons that roamed around; additionally, the fires provided the means by which the required human sacrifice would be presented to the sun god. In enormous wicker baskets, the priests caged both human and animal sacrifices, which they then lowered into the flames. The priests would carefully watch the manner in which the victim died in order to predict whether the future held good or evil.

Trick or Treat is over 2,000 years old. People put food offerings outside their homes so the wandering evil spirits would consume them on their way back to the netherworld. Failure to "treat" these evil spirits might result in a curse.

The American version of Halloween came from Ireland. The potato famine in 1840 brought thousands of immigrants to the USA. With them came the artefacts of their own folk beliefs and customs: goblins, Jack-o'-lanterns, bonfires, apples, nuts, and tricks. In Ireland on 31 October, peasants went from house to house to receive offerings to their Druid god, Muck Olla. This procession stopped at each house to warn the farmer that if he did not provide an offering, misfortune might befall him and his crops.

Frightening costumes. People clothed themselves in the most hideous and terrifying costumes. Huge bonfires were linked to Satan's domain. These bonfires provided the means by which the priests sacrificed the human and animal sacrifices so crucial to Halloween. When the last fires died out, people would race each other down the hills shouting, "The Devil gets the last one down".

Apple games. Apples have long been a token of love and fertility. At Halloween parties, people bobbed for apples in tubs of water. If a boy came up with an apple between his teeth, he was assured of the love of his girl.

Apple seeds were also used to tell fortunes. Peeling an apple in one long piece was supposed to tell a young girl about her future. Owls, bats, cats, and toads are an essential part of Halloween, and were known as "the witch's familiars". A divining familiar was perceived as the species of animal whose shape Satan would assume to aid the witch in divining the future. Other "familiar spirit" shapes include hens, geese, small dogs, rats, butterflies, wasps, crickets, and snails. Celts often hollowed out a turnip and carved a face on it to fool demons. They carried such lanterns to light their way in the dark and to ward off evil spirits. While the turnip continues to be popular in Europe today, the pumpkin has replaced it in America. "Jack" is a nickname for "John", which is a common slang word meaning "man". Jack-O-Lanterns literally means "man with a lantern".

There are many different legends involving Satan and Jack-o'-Lanterns.

November

1:     Satanist High Holy Day (related to Halloween) All Saint's Day, (feast for the saints with no nameday of their own). The Isia: six days of ritual drama commemorating Isis searching for the pieces of Osiris, feast of the netherworlds, parting of the astral veil, resurrection of Osiris.
2:     All Soul's Day (feast in honour of the dead), Day of the Dead (Santeria), Day of the Dead, El Dia De Los Muertos.
4:     Satanic revels.
7:     Rebirth of Osiris.
21–22: Musemass. The Christian church created this day for St Cecilia, goddess of music, who prayed to stay a virgin.

December

5:     Sinterklaas (Holland).
6:     St Nicholas's Day.
12–19: Jewish winter festival of Light, Chanukah, start of the Winter Solstice, animal sacrifice and live burial of victims to celebrate the dark time.
12–13: St. Lucia's Day.
17–22: Saturnalia.
21:    St Thomas Day. Yule. Winter Solstice, fire.
21:    Feast Day, orgies.
22:    Yule/Winter Solstice.
24:    Christmas Eve/Satanic and demon revels/Da Meur/ Grand High Climax.

The Saxon name was Mondranect, the night of mothering. The day is dedicated to the birth of the sun and the goddess Astarte. The following night is celebration of the mother as Sea Mother.

25:    Christmas Day, ascribed to the birth of Jesus, is the birthday of the Sun and Tammuz, the reincarnation of the sun god. Yule, the Winter Solstice of 21st December was moved by the Roman Catholic Church to 25th December. 25th December was also the Roman Saturnalia festival, a time for drinking and feasting. Druids also saw the mistletoe as representing sexuality at this period.

The winter solstice occurs on 21st December, and this is one of the highest pagan/Celtic holidays, since the "New Year" begins after this date for the cult. Special ceremonies are planned to ensure the coming of a new year filled with power, and the return of the sun's lengthening days. In some cults, children are abused by cult members dressed as Santa (anagram for Satan).

Since the sun was experienced as having reversed itself and was now rising in the sky, pagans believed this was a sign that the human sacrifices carried out in Samhain (Halloween) had been accepted by the gods. We continue to connect with these ancient beliefs through some of our Christmas songs.

Christmas Tree: The sacred tree of the winter god; Druids believed the spirit of their gods resided in the tree. Most ancient pagans knew the tree represented Nimrod reincarnated into Tammuz. Pagans also looked upon the tree as a phallic symbol.

Star: pentagram or pentalpha, the five-pointed star, the triple triangle. This is a powerful symbol of Satan, second only to the hexagram. The star is the sacred symbol of Nimrod,

Candles represent the sun god's newly born fire. Pagans the world over love to use candles in their rituals and ceremonies.

Mistletoe is the sacred plant of the Druids, symbolizing pagan blessings of fertility; thus, kissing under the mistletoe is the first step in the reproductive cycle. Witches also use the white berries in potions.

Wreaths are circular, and they represent the female sexual organs. Wreaths are associated with fertility and the "circle of life".

Santa Claus: "Santa" is an anagram for "Satan". In the New Age, the god "Sanat Kamura" is an anagram for "Satan".

Reindeer are horned animals representing the "horned god" or the "stag god" of pagan religion. Santa's traditional number of reindeer in his team is eight; in Satanic gematria, eight is the number of "new beginnings", or the cycle of reincarnation. The Illuminati views the number "eight" as a symbol of their New World Order.

Green and red are the traditional colours of the season, as they are the traditional pagan colours of winter and seen by some groups to be key Satanist colours; red is the colour of blood.

26:     Boxing Day (UK, Canada, Australia, New Zealand). Boxing Day is a day the higher classes gave gifts to the lower classes. Before or on 25th December, people of similar class would exchange gifts to celebrate the Christmas season. Gifts were not exchanged with the lower class until the next day, called Boxing Day. It is also known as St Stephen's Day. Sometimes gifts were put in a box, and breaking the box, or something like a Piggy Bank, would happen. Church used collection boxes to distribute money to the poor on this day.

26:     St Stephen's Day (Scotland).

26–2 January: Hanukkah, Jewish Feast of Lights, Rededication of the Temple.

31:     New Year's Eve.

The eight key dates

Yule/Winter Solstice	22 December
Imbolc/Brigid's Day/Candlemas	2 February
Ostara/Spring	21 March
Beltane	1 May
Midsummer/Alban Hefin	21 June
Lughnasadh/Lammas	1 August
MabonAutumn Equinox	21 September
Samhain/Halloween	31 October

Other triggers

Birthdays come from the Assyro-Babylonian system and were linked to human sacrifice. Dying on a birthday is part of the "neat" way there is an attempt to control nature and time.

This calendar is an aid to looking at triggers linked to belief systems. There are, however, many other triggers linked to aspects of abuse, including, colours, jewels, clothes, eating, drinking, washing, sleeping, having sex, pregnancy and childbirth, blood, loud voices, hospitals, illness, reading, watching films, hearing sirens. In fact, given the enormous number of trigger some people have faced, it is remarkable that they can function in any way.

Some deities

The Babylonian deity Marduk was associated with Mars.

Bel/Baal was the name under which nations were introduced to Marduk.

Marduk/Nimrod has the serpent as his key symbol.

The worship of Nimrod and Semiramis is the key source of pagan religions.

Marduk led the rebellion of gods against Tiamat.

Mother and child, Semiramis and Tammuz, become Isis and Osiris, Venus and Adonis, Madonna and child.

Tammuz became incorporated into Satan.

Beel-Zebub, Lord of the Flies, also means motion and travel in that the fly was restless and darted about.

Ashtar, queen of heaven, kept "male" priestesses known as her faithful "dogs".

Conclusions

Casting the first stone

As the stones weep
Scrubbing at their bloodstains
On the village Square

I am asking the Elders
I am asking the "faithful"
Whose God-face lies
Clenched in their fists
Like a missile

[Valerie Sinason]

All recorded history shows an existence of religious beliefs, dates, and ceremonies. All belief systems have themes of birth, death, sacrifice, and rebirth in common. While there has been a progression in more democratic countries to moving from actual sacrifice to symbolic sacrifice, from blood to wine, there are fundamentalist belief systems and cults that perpetuate primitive modes of functioning. Of course, in times of war, even the most morally advanced nations revert to primitive modes of functioning.

The written tenets of most world religions, or rather, the all-too-human cultures they are embedded in, include approval for actions that are against twenty-first century law and basic child protection procedures. However, the slow progression to deities of loving attachment has allowed progress. Those who are frozen into the literal word are like the emotional part in a DID system, condemned to a perpetual darkness of shame, pain, and punishment, where a deity of light and love does not appear.

We must note that Satanism is now a legal belief system recognized by the British Government, and most Satanists would not hurt anyone and are often refugees from hell-based branches of Christianity from which they need a defence.

We also need to note that people in cultures without a deity or deities hurt others, and people with deities hurt others. We are a primitive species passing on our trauma. No single belief is the cause of ritual pain.

However, fascism plus religion carries an extra terror, as it gives a sense of hopelessness and slavery even after death.

The use and perversion of religions and other beliefs for the purpose of hurting children and adults is something that we all need to be watchful over.

* * *

With thanks to the BBC multifaith calendar, which provides dates for Bahai, Buddhist, Christian, Hindu, Jain, Jewish, Muslim, Pagan, Rastafari, Shinto, Sikh, Zorostrian, and to Wikopedia, Survivorship.org, Ritual Abuse Dates, and to the survivors from all over the world who have helped me with this by sending in information.

The dates and information provided in this booklet come from survivors all over the world. Where information has been provided from the Internet a source is given.

This calendar is a work in progress and we welcome further additions.

References

Hale, R., & Sinason, V. (1994). Internal and external reality: establishing parameters. In: V. Sinason (Ed.), *Treating Survivors of Satanist Abuse* (pp. 274–284). London: Routledge.

Noblitt, R., & Perskin Noblitt, P. (2008). *Ritual Abuse in the 21st Century*. Bandon, OR: Robert D. Reed.

Sinason, V. (Ed.) (1994). *Treating Survivors of Satanist Abuse* (pp. 274–284). London: Routledge.

Sinason, V. (2008). From social conditioning to mind control. In: A. Sachs & G. Galton (Eds.), *Forensic Aspects of Dissociative Identity Disorder* (pp. 167–185). London: Karnac.

CHAPTER TWO

"An evil cradling"? Cult practices and the manipulation of attachment needs in ritual abuse

Rachel Wingfield Schwartz

I n his remarkable autobiographical account of his years held as a hostage in Beirut, Brian Keenan describes his captivity and his relationship to his captors as "an evil cradling":

> My days passed in a slow, gentle delirium; like the comfort and reassurance that a child must feel as its mother rocks and sings it a lullaby. I looked wildly at a dead insect in my cell, hanging in its cocoon. I felt a strange contentment. I felt no desire to leave this place. I found myself thinking with the shadows of panic rising in me that I was not ready to leave, that I did not want to leave. I began to dread my freedom, if it should come. [Keenan, 1993, p. 73]

In this account, Keenan enables us to begin to understand that being enfolded, cradled in this cocoon of captivity, evil though it may be, begins to present a kind of safety for the captive, the alternative to which-escape—seems to threaten only terror and the unknown. The survivors of ritual abuse and mind control that we will talk about over the course of this Conference grew up within an evil cradling; within families and cults who set out to make it impossible for them to ever escape; impossible for them to ever break the psychological bonds with their abusers, bonds carefully welded within a cocoon of torture and programming.

I was reminded, by Keenan's words, of a client of mine, a ritual abuse survivor who described her relationship with her mother— one of the main perpetrators of her abuse. She told me:

> I would sit for hours, often, just staring at her face or preferably stroking her arm or feeling her stroke mine. I got such a sense of security just being able to stare at her and feel her body next to mine. The rest of the world went away. Like we were in a bubble together. Even in to my twenties I would still sit on her knee, and I would still scream and shout sometimes if she left the room. It's years since I've seen her, but I still wake up crying for my mummy in the night. Part of me is desperate just to have the comfort of touching her again. She always told me I would never be able to live without her and even now I sometimes think she might be right.

The theme of this book is the manipulation of attachment needs. I think this is a key to understanding the traumatic experience of people ritually abused in cults. I want to write from the perspective of being an attachment-based therapist and explore some of what I have learnt over the years from survivors about the use and abuse of the attachment system by perpetrators within ritual abuse. I also want to think about what survivors need relationally from psychotherapy if recovery is to be possible, and what it means to try to build a new working model of attachment in therapy when someone has a history of that need for attachment being so distorted and manipulated. To address these issues, I am going to focus on my work over a period of eight years with a young woman I am going to call Jodi, who was a survivor of ritual abuse and mind control.

Jodi

Jodi was referred to me by a colleague, who assured me she would not be a long-term client and did not have severe trauma in her history. She had a life crisis she needed to talk over with someone. That was all. Her brother had recently been diagnosed with schizophrenia and she was feeling very concerned and distressed about him. She needed someone to talk to. However, I have found, as many of you may have, too, that once you have started working clinically around ritual abuse it tends to find you wherever you go.

Jodi arrived punctually for her first session, and was immediately charming. She had found the journey easy, she loved the house, she was so grateful to me for seeing her. She told me she was twenty-four years old, a drama student at a prestigious school, and she still lived with her family—her parents, and her younger brother, who was Jodi's main focus in this session. As Jodi talked about her brother's recent breakdown, and began to describe the panic she had been experiencing, I found myself starting to feel more and more anxious. Jodi was talking calmly, but I became aware that the feelings were intensifying; I was not so much anxious any more, but terrified. I could feel myself starting to hyperventilate. For a brief moment, I wondered if I was safe with her, or if she was about to attack me. The body countertransference hit me so rapidly and so powerfully I was literally struggling for breath, and struggling even harder to regulate myself. I needed to slow myself down enough to begin to unravel what was happening.

I said to Jodi, "As you were talking, I started feeling terrible anxiety in my body. Then I felt terrified and was struggling to breathe. I think you were letting me know how frightened you are. Is that right?"

She looked at me silently, and after a little while, nodded.

The feelings in my body started to recede, my breathing calmed down and so did the feelings of terror. Jodi, on the other hand, began to struggle. She tried to continue talking about her brother, but she could not focus, could not breathe properly, and was moving agitatedly in her chair. I could feel she could not bear to sit with me in the room for another minute and abruptly I got out of my chair, saying I was going to get her a glass of water, and left the room. I was puzzled about this; I had never done this in the middle of a session with a client before, but I also felt absolutely certain that it was the right thing to do, that she could not have coped with my presence any longer. When I returned, she was calmer, but different. She could not look at me, spoke in a gentle, halting voice, and tried to explain that she had been having trouble recently "losing herself"; as she described it, the fear would come, and then she would have no sense of where she was, or what was happening.

Although I was not sure what was triggering these feelings of fear, I had no doubt that I was sitting with an extremely terrorized young woman and my feelings also left me wondering if she had experienced violence. These were feelings I was familiar with when working with people who were severely traumatized.

Jodi decided she would commit to undertaking therapy, and arranged to see me twice weekly, although, over the eight years of our work together, she was to increase to four times weekly sessions. The early months were dominated by continuing intense shifts in states, the room drenched in fear, a sense of immanent violence pervading the sessions, with intermittent periods of us both being drawn in to calm, hypnotic, trance-like states. Jodi spoke in these sessions about her great concern and attachment to her brother. Jodi felt his vulnerability acutely and cited him as a key reason why she had not been able to leave home, despite being offered student accommodation at her drama school. Jodi also spoke in these sessions about her relationship with her mother. "We're joined," she said, "if she dies, I die. We're one person." When Jodi spoke about her mother, I would feel an intense sense of suffocation, alongside the depth of her ambivalence: of her desperately needing to be with her mother, to be in constant phone contact when she was away at school for the day, coupled with a rage and a desire to attack her mother.

In attachment terms, Jodi was presenting with classic features of disorganized/disorientated infants. She moved in and out of seemingly contradictory states, both in sessions and in relation to her mother. Longing for contact could be followed by becoming frozen or frightened when the contact became available. Being with Jodi was being with the ongoing, terrible experience of fright without solution; the terror was palpable, the strategies for managing it never anything more than a temporary escape into dissociation.

She felt to me like an occupied person, her mind and body colonized by violent and terrifying others from whom it was only possible to escape through dissociative trance states. These states grew more dominant as we continued the work, and Jodi would "trance out", as she called it, in sessions, lying on the couch drifting between associations, in a dream-like state, and often talking to me in a child's voice.

A pattern began to emerge between us that whenever Jodi took a step towards trusting me, she would follow up in the next session with an attack. This happened when there were reminders that we were becoming attached: for example, a break, or a missed session, or a feeling of connection.

We both survived Jodi's attacks. And I felt for Jodi an emerging sense of "going on being". I was careful to attune and respond to her levels of distress and fear, without coming any closer than that Jodi could bear.

It took this period of becoming "secure enough" in the relationship with me, and in the world, before Jodi was able to talk to me directly about the abuse in her family or about the ritual abuse. She began by talking to me about her father. He had sexually abused her from as far back as she could remember. He still sometimes came to her room at night to have sex with her. Jodi found herself unable to say no. At times Jodi could not find words to tell me what her father had done to her: in a child's voice she would start to try to speak, crying quietly, and would then make a scribbling movement with her hand as though to say, I need a pen, I need to write this. When she did write, it would just be words: rape, penis, mouth, bleeding. We sat together with tears in our eyes as she passed me a drawing of a child with a kitchen implement being pushed into her bottom and then later a knife. Jodi and I shared together this feeling of grief and sorrow for her child self, for how terrified she still was as she began to speak out about this. There was a feeling of deep closeness and connection in the session, and at the end Jodi smiled shakily and said thank you.

I had expected that there might be a backlash after this session, but had not anticipated the extent of it.

Jodi arrived at the next session and told me she had come to say goodbye, she could not come to therapy any more. She said she had also informed her drama school that she would not be coming back. She needed to get a job and get on with her life. She had no idea why she had said the things she did last week—her father would never abuse her. She was a liar. She was wasting my time.

As Jodi spoke I was aware of another part of her being present: it was as though I could hear that part of her crying and crying, in terrible pain and despair. I responded to that part of Jodi. "Jodi, I can feel someone inside crying and crying as though they will never be able to stop. That person's heart is broken. I think we need to give her chance to speak."

Jodi shook her head, but I saw her eyes begin to fill with tears. "I can't tell you, I can't tell you," she said. For fifteen minutes we sat in silence, with tears pouring down Jodi's face, breathing slowly together. At one point, I broke the silence and said, "It's OK, just take your time. I'll be here for you, whatever it is." "I can't tell you because it's to do with you," she said. "It will hurt you." After more silence, and several attempts, Jodi was able to tell me that she had seen my cat in the garden on the way in to the session. She said she knew that if she came to see me again, she would have to kill my cat. She had an image in her head, of my cat split open, her insides taken out and displayed next to her. In the image, the blood was all over Jodi's hands. "I can smell the blood," she kept saying, "I can smell it and taste it in my mouth." As she said this, she went white and began to look nauseous. I could feel myself starting to feel faint in response, the vomit rising in my throat, and I was not certain I would be able to stop myself throwing up in the room. Jodi beat me to it, rushing out of her seat to the bathroom, saying, "I'm going to be sick." She arrived back in the room after being sick, pale and dazed. I asked her, "Jodi, when you were young, did you have any pets?" She nodded. "I had a rabbit. Then I had a kitten. And later a pet dog." What happened to them? She looked at me. "I don't know." "Perhaps someone inside knows," I suggested. "Why don't you ask?" She closed her eyes and when she opened them again, a small but lively voice said to me, "I know what happened to Jasmine, our rabbit. She was mine." I recognized this little one: I had met her before, and she had been a big help to Jodi and me in the therapy so far. "Hello Josie," I said. "Would you be able to tell me about Jasmine?" Josie told me that Jasmine was Jodi's pet when she was four years old, and that she had been given to Jodi by her grandmother as a special present. Josie looked after Jasmine and would play with her in the garden for hours. Then, one evening, she had arrived home from school and her mother had been cooking dinner. Jodi had asked what was for dinner but had been told to be quiet and to wash her hands ready for the meal. As Jodi had her first bites of the stew her mother had cooked, her father began to laugh. "Jasmine won't be playing with you much now," he had said. At first, Jodi has refused to believe it. She had shouted at her father, told him he was lying. She ran down to the hutch and found Jasmine missing. Her mother insisted she come back to the table. "You are going to finish every last mouthful on that plate," her mother had told her. Jodi sat there for hours, trying to swallow through her tears and through rising vomit. When she did not finish her plate before going to bed she was forced to eat the stew cold for breakfast the next morning.

I felt in shock as she told me this story, struggling to imagine how a child could bear this. But Josie said brightly, "But that wasn't so bad. It wasn't as bad as when we had to kill the kitten." A few years later, at the age of seven, Jodi had been allowed to keep a kitten, which had turned up as a stray in their garden. Jodi said the kitten was her best friend. When she wanted to escape her father's abuse and her mother's rages, she would hide in the garden shed with Kitty, playing or just falling asleep with Kitty curled up beside her or in her lap. One afternoon, her mother found her asleep in there with Kitty and told her to bring the cat into the house. She said that Jodi had been a bad girl. She had been telling lies. That her mother knew she had been thinking bad thoughts about her family: that she was angry with them, that she hated them. She said that Kitty would have to be punished: Jodi had been so bad, that she had caused Kitty to have to be hurt. Jodi had a choice. Either her mother would kill Kitty slowly, or Jodi could kill her quickly so that she would not feel too much pain. Jodi sobbed and begged her mother to hurt her instead of Kitty. But her mother said no: when Jodi was bad, it was the things that she cared about that would be punished. That was what happened if you were bad inside, and you loved something or someone. As Jodi's mother began to slowly torture Kitty, Jodi did break down and agree to kill Kitty. She sat in my consulting room as an adult, with tears pouring down her face, and said, "It broke my heart. It was like part of me died inside. I never felt the same again. I knew that I was bad deep down and that my badness would take everything and everyone away from me that I cared about."

We were able to understand from this why Jodi had been so afraid that our closeness in the previous session, and her disclosure of her father's abuse, would mean that she would have to hurt me in some way and why this had become focused on my cat. Over time, these fears were to re-emerge many times, and often precipitated a memory of being made to believe, programmed to believe, that if she grew attached to anyone other than specific cult members, she would lose them, and also that she would put them and herself in danger.

After this, Jodi and I had a period of intense closeness. At times, the intimacy in the sessions felt almost exhilarating. Warm, loving feelings were often present as she shyly shared her successes at drama school and allowed more and more of her people inside to come and meet me and spend time with me. Again, we were to face a backlash. Jodi came into the session one day and told me coldly that she was sick of my yucky, sickly, nicey-nice ways. That she knew what I was up to, and she knew what I was really after. I was sick and a pervert, just like everyone else. I was only pretending to care about her. I asked her where this had come from: she insisted it had not come from anywhere, she was just making sure I knew that I could not mess her about or play games with her. This went on for several sessions, as I tried to understand where this had come from and endeavoured to find out if anyone else in the system knew what had happened. Eventually, with much shame, an adult in her system explained that her family and "they"—she did not specify who "they" were at this stage—had told her that I was only being nice to her to get her to have sex with me, that in the end, everybody wanted something, and that was clearly what I wanted.

She told me that she had believed this because some people inside, particularly the children, did not understand about sex. They did not understand that there were relationships where two people were not supposed to have sex. This led to her describing to me how father would take her to see men as a child, his friends or other family members, and tell her to have sex with them. "Sometimes they paid him." It then also enabled her to tell me more about her relationship with her mother.

Jodi and her mother had often slept in the same bed since Jodi was a child and this had stopped only recently, at Jodi's instigation. "She taught me how to give her orgasms when I was just little. She used to get me to look at porn sometimes too, to show me what to do. It made me feel special to her. Like we had a special relationship that no one could ever break into. She always told me that we were joined and that she could read my mind. She would do games and experiments with me to prove she could read it. She told me I belonged to her, I was part of her, that the two of us would be together in the afterlife, too. That there would never be anyone else in my life who could know me and love me like she did, because I had come from inside her and I belonged inside her."

As we talked more about Jodi's mother and her hold over Jodi, it became clear that her mother had been able to manipulate Jodi's terrible fear of not being in proximity to her, of needing her presence, alongside Jodi's enormous sense of loyalty to her mother. Jodi's attachment to her mother had been fused with training— training which was really torture—which taught Jodi to believe that her mother had power over her life and death and controlled her internal world. This training had also heightened Jodi's attachment to her mother.

Jodi recalled incidents from early in her childhood, in which her mother would put her in life and death situations and then seemingly rescue her from them, just in time. On one occasion, her mother had locked her in a trunk and shut her in the cellar where, she said, no one would hear Jodi if she screamed. In the trunk with Jodi, she put insects, including maggots, of which Jodi was particularly frightened. Jodi remembers the panic and the terror, the feelings of suffocation and the certainty she would die. Gradually, she said, she gave up—just found herself drifting in a dissociated space, aware she could barely breathe any longer. At that point, in Jodi's memory, her mother opened the trunk and pulled her out, sobbing, asking Jodi how she had ended up being locked in trunk, telling Jodi she loved her desperately and no matter where Jodi got lost, she would always find her. However bad things got for Jodi, she would always save her.

In *Trauma and Recovery*, Judith Herman describes the process of "pair bonding" between victim and perpetrator. She explains,

> This is the traumatic bonding that occurs in hostages and survivors of abuse who come to view their captors as saviours. . . . The repeated experience of terror and reprieve, especially within the isolated context of a love relationship, may result in a feeling of intense, almost worshipful dependence upon an all-powerful godlike authority. Some victims speak of entering a kind of exclusive, almost delusional world, embracing the grandiose belief

system of the perpetrator and voluntarily suppressing their own doubts as a proof of loyalty and submission. Similar experiences are regularly reported by people who have been inducted into totalitarian religious cults. [1992, p. 92]

We see here that Satanist cults are able to manipulate these psychic susceptibilities as a result of bonding through extreme trauma, and draw the victim in to wider submission and loyalty to the group's belief system.

Our attachment system is most activated when we are in danger, and the intensity of being rescued from these near-death experiences reinforced the desperate clinging nature of Jodi's attachment to her mother. She literally believed that her continued survival depended on proximity to her mother, and that leaving home, leaving her, would mean death. Jodi described how her mother had reinforced this childhood magical thinking through drawing Jodi in to a supernatural belief system, a form of witchcraft through which her mother was able to make Jodi believe that shat she had claimed her soul and that terrible death and eternal torment would result if she tried to leave her mother. "She possessed my soul through a spell. The punishment would be eternal if I left her."

At this stage, Jodi began to talk more about the involvement of the wider cult in her life. She started to paint in sessions when she could not find words for what had happened to her at the hands of other cult members, and with the involvement of her parents. This set of paintings and drawings brought a new atmosphere to the room—chilling, sinister, full of terror and sadism. There were paintings of Jodi's mother gagging her, holding a knife to her feet, threatening to cut them off, pictures of blood, axes, knives, scissors, blindfolds, electroshocks, being hung upside down, strangled, and having her stomach cut open. As Jodi free-associated on this, she was able to communicate with the people inside who had drawn the pictures, and through them we learned more about the programmes of torture she had gone through to enforce her loyalty to the cult. During this period, in my notes I wrote, "nausea, blood, semen, vomit, sweat: the room reeks of them. Like it's pouring down the walls".

From early in her childhood, Jodi had been encouraged to make particular friendships with adults or other children in the cult. These were carefully fostered, as with her earlier relationships with her pets, with the clear intention of demonstrating to Jodi that the cult had control over the making and breaking of her attachment bonds. Jodi described how, from an early age, her attachments to other children were used to manipulate her into doing things for the cult that she otherwise resisted doing. She had memories of being forced to watch one of her friends being abused, and being told that unless she carried out an act she shrank from, such as killing an animal, or abusing another child, the abuse of her friend would continue, or they would be tortured. At times, she would be told that unless she tortured her friend, they would be killed. Having seen these people kill, Jodi said she absolutely believed they would make good their threats. She believed them capable of anything. Jodi's most painful memories at this time involved her younger brother, who was now schizophrenic. Jodi said, "He was littler than me, and I was always so frightened for him—he never seemed to do things right, he was always getting punished. They used to make me hurt him—they would say, 'we're going to cut out his guts unless you hurt him or unless you abuse him'. Sometimes I refused, but then they would torture him and make me watch and I would beg them to stop. Then I had to do what they told me. Every time I look at him now, I know it's my fault that he's so ill, that he keeps breaking down. I should have found a way to protect him or to get him out of there. I was older than him, he depended on me."

Unsurprisingly, Jodi's relationship with me created enormous conflict inside her. I was seen as a threatening force. Some people inside feared I was luring Jodi in to a trap, but more people felt I was dangerous because I was threatening her attachment to her mother. There were particular people inside who had been created by her mother and by the cult, who believed it was their role to ensure Jodi's loyalty to her mother at all costs: these were programmed alters, who tried desperately to sabotage Jodi's relationship with me. Others inside felt that even if she survived separating from her mother, internally she would be alone forever. Only the others in the cult could understand her, would not reject her for doing the things she had done. They knew she was special and powerful, and also would not be disgusted by her.

All cults instil these feelings in their members, but it is particularly effective in ritual abuse, because the sense of being other and separate is brought about through breaking the very boundaries and taboos of what it means to be human. Cannibalism, drinking blood, eating and drinking faeces and urine, committing incest and murder—these acts contravene what anthropologists would describe to us as the boundaries that cultures use to define being human and being a member of human society. Jodi did not only feel she was different from other people, but that she would not even be included or accepted as a member of human society. This meant that the cult became the only society of which she could be part.

None the less, through our regular sessions and her experience of being attuned to, Jodi was beginning to feel as if she might be able to belong to another world, to this world. The work we had done to help her regulate her core self functions was enabling her to participate in life at college. Talking about her mother's abuse of her enabled Jodi to begin to separate from her mother. She was also working part-time to achieve some financial independence for the first time. She was making friends and she was doing well in her classes. She rarely lost time now, and this gave her a sense of being part of the world that she had never had before.

What was not clear to us was how safe Jodi was from cult abuse in the present. The fact that Jodi was not losing much time seemed hopeful. But we began to receive communications from the others inside that she still was not safe. For the first time, Jodi announced that she was going to leave home. The next phase of the therapy was a battle for Jodi to make this happen.

In November, after months of tumultuous sessions and sadistic attacks on me and the therapy, Jodi moved out. Internally, she was then immediately flooded by persecutory cult voices: lying to her, seductive, tormenting her constantly, telling her she had to be punished. Jodi was making threats to go back, and saying she could not break contact.

As Judith Herman describes,

> the sense that the perpetrator is still present, even after liberation, signifies a major constellation in the victim's relational world. The enforced relationship during captivity, becomes part of the victim's inner life. . . . In the case of sexual, domestic and religious cult prisoners, this continued relationship may take a more ambivalent form: the victim may continue to fear her former captor and to

expect that he will eventually hunt her down, but she may also feel empty, confused and worthless without him. [1992, p. 91]

It felt as if Jodi was stuck at this point forever. It was only possible for a shift to occur through an enactment in the transference–countertransference relationship. I was by this point feeling devoured, what Valerie Sinason calls the cannibalistic countertransference; Jodi's persecution and abuse in the sessions and constant pushing of boundaries between sessions were making me feel bullied, controlled, and victimized. I realized that *I* had to liberate myself from Jodi's internal abusers: that anything else would lock us into a sadomasochistic re-enactment, a home from home for Jodi where relationships were again as they were in the cult, only this time I was the victim. I told Jodi I felt unable to continue the work unless the bullying stopped and the constant attacks on me and the therapy stopped; I found my subjectivity, and stood up to her persecutors. She knew I meant it. Having experienced *me* doing this enabled Jodi to do it, too. She broke contact with her family and the cult.

This was then followed by changes as a result of a new strategy inside to co-operate and negotiate—the abusers were no longer in control inside or out.

The atmosphere in the sessions was often one of excitement, intimacy, and intense emotion. This raised Jodi's fear of sexuality and an intense fear of loving me. Having love in her life at all felt like an acceptance that she deserved love, which, in turn, meant that she was ceasing to receive the punishment she felt she required; it was betraying her loyalty to the cult and to her mother, and, more significantly, betraying those she had been involved in abusing or killing.

Jodi reached the point where she knew inside herself that she had to try to work through the guilt and self-hate about being made to be a perpetrator. When Jodi had reached puberty, as with all female ritual abuse survivors, she was forced to kill her baby, whose birth had been prematurely induced by the cult doctor. Did Jodi remember being pregnant? She described holding the baby in her arms for a few moments after the birth, just before the killing. As a thirteen-year-old, powerless to prevent the killing, she made a bargain with herself. She and the baby would stay frozen in the moment forever. Although she could not save her baby, in order to deal with her remorse she swore to herself that she would love the child forever and never share that love with anyone else or feel it again: in that way, she could make the baby's short life have a meaning. This meant that in therapy she fought and battled against the growing loving feelings for me, and repeatedly attacked the relationship, as it felt like a profound betrayal and abandonment of her baby.

Becoming conscious of this horrific event enabled Jodi to connect with the person inside, frozen in time, still holding the baby. A great deal of negotiation and communication went on inside, until it was agreed internally that it was time to let the baby inside be taken to heaven to be with God. We planned carefully for the session in which this was to happen. Jodi brought some flowers for the baby, and some bulbs for us to plant outside, to mark her loss. Inside, some of her people came and put their arms around the Jodi who was still holding the baby. They gently held her, while they took the baby from her. Tears were pouring down Jodi's face. "It's time now," she said. They took the baby to a bridge, which passed outside of the system, into another world outside of her. Jodi carefully laid the baby on a hillside filled with flowers on the other side of the bridge. Then the little group said goodbye, and walked back together over the bridge, holding up the part of her that had been frozen but who was now collapsing under the weight of the tears, the pain of knowing that her baby was gone, and this loss could never be undone.

This proved to be a turning point for Jodi in allowing herself to accept that the past happened and can never be changed. She has to live in the present, however much pain there has been. It was time for a life outside the cult.

There was, however, one final and fundamental conflict around attachment still to be faced. Jodi was finally able to let her dead baby go, but her brother was very much alive. He was still living at home, and Jodi did not know the extent of his continued involvement with the cult. As her brother's birthday approached, we noticed a dramatic deterioration in Jodi's state. She began damaging the relationships and people in her life and things that mattered to her again. She even lost some time again, coming to and finding she had cut herself. She dreamed about a birthday cake and we were able to make the connection with her brother. As Jodi began to face her profound feelings of survivor guilt, for being able to leave when he could not, at times she felt despair. It began to feel that we were stuck again: she could not believe that it would ever be all right for her to have her freedom and her life, knowing that she had left him behind. She felt that doing this would mean that the cult was right: she was not human, inside she was just selfish, and she had proved it time and again when she harmed others to save herself.

She began to feel drawn back to contacting the family. Perhaps she could prove that she did care about someone else more than herself. In desperation, I reviewed my learning about survivor guilt and read everything I could lay my hands on to try to understand what might help Jodi. What did feel clear to me was that she needed some sense of not being alone with this, of belonging to a community of other trauma survivors who could assure her that it did not rob her of humanity to live and move on. She also needed to find a way to understand that although she wanted to save her brother, she could not. Only he could find his way out, and that might never happen.

In my reading, I came across Brian Keenan's *An Evil Cradling*, with which I started this paper. During his four years in captivity, Brian Keenan was held in a cell with journalist John McCarthy. He recognized that it was this relationship with John that enabled him to survive and to hold on to his sanity.

He feels he owes his life to John, and vice versa. Then the day comes when he is told he is going to be released. This means leaving John behind. He is left with the dilemma of refusing his freedom, or staying behind in captivity with John. Keenan describes his internal battle over this, and his eventual realization that to choose to remain in captivity would be a betrayal of his relationship with John and would diminish what they had fought for together.

He writes,

> I remember every moment of my time alone, my time with John and with those other captives. And I remember how we first met, our relationship, the kinds of needs I had of John and he of me. And how we sought always to give and take, always thinking of the other. And as I review it all, all that wonder, I see his face stare in mine. I had watched this man grow. And I know that if in my defiance I walk back in to that room and have myself chained, refusing

to go home, I will have diminished our relationship. I cannot do this. I know that in going free I will free him. I know that the deep bond our captivity has given us will be shattered if I return. Our respect for each other demands of each that we take our freedom when it comes. [1993, p. 292]

When Jodi read these words, something began to release inside her. She could understand why Brian Keenan had made the choice that he had. She did not feel he was a bad person for leaving John behind. She wept many tears, and wrote her brother long letters she could never send, but she resolved in herself that she had to find a way to say goodbye to him. She visited a park they had played in as children and read out loud Brian Keenan's words and a poem she had written to say goodbye to her brother. She brought me the poem afterwards and asked me to keep it. "You know, in a way no one else could, what it means to me to leave him. You know I loved him. Despite everything they did to try to stop me from believing I was capable of loving anyone. You know I am capable of love. You know this because you know I feel love for you."

Jodi was right. They were not able to destroy her capacity to love, or her connection to it. They manipulated her need for attachment, but, ultimately, it was her ability to attach and her ability to build a new working model of attachment that enabled her to escape them. Through our relationship, Jodi has internalized a sense of being loveable, of being able to relate, of being able to function in this world. We worked together for eight years; five years has passed since then. Jodi now has a well-paid, successful job in theatre, friendships, and a loving long-term relationship with a partner. I want to finish with a quote from a letter I received from Jodi after her therapy ended.

We're finding it a challenge to become part of normal life now outside of the cult: no therapy, and without constant emergencies, adrenaline, urgency. But I'm also aware I'm ready for civilian life. I'm being demobbed. Sometimes the fighters from the past get worried they won't be wanted anymore or needed. A bit like a Mad-Eye Moody in Harry Potter: a bit OTT, too suspicious, spotting dark wizards everywhere. But he's also someone who sees unpleasant truths that other people would rather not see. So he's important, and those people in me are important. They've been through so much. They deserve to be part of my life in this world now.

I think of you often, and I know you will be there for me if I need you. I have such strong feelings of love for people I'm close to: every time I'm glad to see someone, or I hug someone, or I make love with my partner, I know somewhere deep inside that I survived what they did to me. I don't treat people the way they did. I would never make that choice. It makes me feel whole.

And you know, often now, I can actually FEEL that it's all me, and all of me is here, us together. And it's my life now, no one else's. All the supernatural stuff is gone, and rain is just rain and not acid; and lightening is just a natural phenomenon and not an attack or electric shock torture. And I am me. In real time.

References

Herman, J. (1992). *Trauma and Recovery*. New York: Basic Books.
Keenan, B. (1993). *An Evil Cradling*. London: Vintage.

CHAPTER THREE

Torture-based mind control: psychological mechanisms and psychotherapeutic approaches to overcoming mind control

Ellen P. Lacter

"Can we get control of an individual to the point where he will do our bidding against his will and even against such fundamental laws of nature such as self-preservation?"

(CIA Document, Project ARTICHOKE, MORI ID 144686, 1952)

Psychological mechanisms

My goal in this chapter is to analyse through established psychological principles how torture-based mind control programming is installed and exerts continued control over victims.

It is painfully humbling to study mind control. The secrets of how it "works" are buried deeply in the minds of survivors whose mental registration of the process was originally impaired by torture, drugs, smoke and mirrors, and dissociative processes, both defensive and effected by abuser manipulation, and whose capacity to later recall and reveal this trauma is limited by terror, abuser subterfuge, and the capacity of the therapist to bear witness to such calculated abuse. Further complicating this study is the variation in methods and forms of mind control reported by survivors.

I will present patterns I have observed for further exploration. My primary data is my work with survivor clients, depth interviews of other survivors, including many psychologist-survivors, interviews with colleagues treating survivors, and written accounts by survivors, most of whom I have interviewed and found credible. I am particularly indebted to Dr Hans Ulrich Gresch, German psychologist, cold war mind control survivor, and author of a book on mind control (Gresch, 2010), for his generous correspondence with me on his experiences as a victim and his insights into mind control as a scholar.

Working definition of torture-based mind control

I define torture-based mind control as the systematic application of (1) acute torture, including pain, terror, drugs, electroshock, sensory deprivation, oxygen deprivation, cold, heat, spinning, brain stimulation, and near-death, and (2), conditioning, including coercive hypnosis, directives, illusions (staged tricks, film, stories), spiritual threats, manipulation of attachment needs, and classical, operant, and fear conditioning, to coerce victims to form altered mental states, including (a) hyper-attentive blank slate (tabula rasa) mental states that arise spontaneously in response to perceived threat to physical survival, and are completely attuned to external stimuli, ready to do whatever is needed to survive; (b) self-states that spontaneously form in response to threat to psychic survival, that is, levels of mental anguish that exceed the tolerance of all previously existing ego states, and that are mentally registered apart (dissociated) from previously existing ego-states; (c) ego-states that develop more gradually through conditioning, all three of which are subjected to "programmer" strategies to define, control, and "install" within them perceptions, beliefs, fear, pain, directives, information, triggers, and behaviours, to force victims to do, feel, think, and perceive things for the purposes of the programmer, including execution of acts that violate the victims' volition, principles, and instinct for self-preservation, and to cause ego-states that usually have executive control of mental functions (the host, front, or apparently normal personality) to have no conscious memory for the torture, conditioning, programming, controlled ego-states, or executed programmed behaviours. (Note: In the field of "torture-based mind-control", this term is generally synonymous with "torture-based" or "trauma-based", followed by "mind control programming" or "programming".)

My proposed definition refers to both *self-states* and *ego-states*. *Self-state* is the broader term, including *self-states* that have minimal sense of self or self-agency, such as torture-induced fragmentary self-states that register pain and terror internally, largely separate from higher cognitive processing and with a bare sense of "me". *Ego-state* refers to a self-state with significant self-identification and self-agency, often referred to as an *alter, dissociated identity* or *personality* in the literature on dissociative identity disorder (DID).

The term "host" refers to the ego-state that is usually experienced as "me", that usually spends the most time in executive control of mental functions and behaviour, and that is more aware of benign circumstances than past or present trauma. Some individuals have more than one host or "front" ego-state. In the literature on dissociative disorders, the term "host" is also often referred to as the apparently normal personality (ANP) (van der Hart, Nijenhuis, & Steele, 2006).

The term "executive control" refers to the implementation of mental functions, otherwise known as "executive functions", that enable goal-directed thought and behaviour, including self-awareness, motivation, volition, initiation, planning, purposive action, and self-regulation, which relies on monitoring, shifting, inhibiting, and self-correcting, functions primarily attributed to the frontal lobes, specifically the prefrontal cortex (Lezak, 1995).

Torture-based mind control is practised by individuals and groups who seek to maximally control and exploit others, particularly children. Included are practitioners of abusive religious rituals (e.g., Satanism and abusive witchcraft), organized crimes against children (child pornography, prostitution, and trafficking), and groups with political, military, and espionage agendas.

Survivors commonly report torture using electroshock, spinning, isolation, confinement (cages, coffins, etc.), sexual abuse, beatings (especially to the head), hanging or pulling with ropes and chains, suffocation, drowning, being held over fire, blinding or flashing light, forced ingestion of blood, urine, faeces, flesh, etc., hunger, thirst, sleep deprivation, sensory deprivation, submersion in ice water, drugs to induce paralysis, pain, confusion, amnesia, etc., application of snakes, spiders, maggots, rats, etc., and being forced to perform or witness abuse, torture and sacrifice of people and animals.

Mind control phenomena reported by survivors

Survivor accounts are the primary source material on torture-based mind control. Critics say this is untrustworthy data. However, torture is criminal internationally, and its effects cannot be directly studied.

Clinicians assess the reliability of survivor accounts based on narrative coherence, goodness of fit between symptoms and reported history, diagnosis of a trauma disorder, differential diagnosis (Lacter & Lehman, 2008), and from multiple sources of corroboration from other survivors.

I have reviewed three lengthy written narratives about torture-based mind control:

1.   Svali (pseudonym): How the cult programs people (1996);
2.   Trish Fotheringham: Patterns in mind-control: a first person account (2008) (Fotheringham reports not having read any other survivor accounts when she wrote her chapter);
3.   Anonymous survivor: Kabbalah-training (provided by a therapist colleague, 2008).

Although these three accounts are very different, each includes abuser aptitude testing of newborns, training infants to dissociate, bonding infants to trainers, destroying all sources of comfort, torture to induce blank-slate self-states (Fotheringham described this in interviews, not in her chapter), developing and categorizing self-states by colour, spinning torture, all-seeing eyes, suicide programming, programming using illusions such as film, and staged dramas to create internal landscapes (or inner worlds).

Some of the strongest corroborative evidence for mind control is a 2007 internet survey in which 1471 people from at least forty countries responded as survivors to *the Extreme Abuse Survey* (EAS) (Becker, Karriker, Overkamp, & Rutz, 2007).

The following list of reported mind control phenomena incorporates a sampling of the EAS findings.

1. Torture to induce the formation of receptive/programmable dissociated self-states. Of 1012 EAS respondents who replied to the item: "My perpetrator(s) deliberately created/programmed dissociative states of mind (such as alters, personalities, ego-states) in me," 640 (63%) said "Yes."

2. Torture to influence the host with no conscious awareness. The host experiences unexplained behavioural compulsions to perform particular behaviours, and programmed self-states take executive control to follow programmed directives, unbeknown to the host.

3. The perception of "structures", that is, mental representations of objects, usually inanimate, in the body or internal landscape in the mind. Often-reported structures include buildings, walls, containers, grids, computers, and devices of torture. Structures often serve organizational purposes for programmers, such as containing groups of self-states that serve particular functions, storing files of information, serving as barriers (walls, caps, seals) to separate groups of self-states, and hiding deeper levels of programming and structures. Dissociated self-states perceive themselves as trapped behind, within, or attached to structures, often reliving the pain, suffocation, electroshock, etc., used to "install" the structure.

4. Perceived explosive devices, electroshock wires and devices, and vials capable of releasing toxins and drugs, in the body of specific self-states, or in the internal landscape, to control behaviour.

5. Perceived internal monitoring devices to watch or "read" and transmit thoughts, e.g., all-seeing eyes, microphones, and microchips.

6. The perception of internal programmers, abusers, demons, and human spirits, to watch and control the victim. Of 996 EAS respondents who replied to the item: "Perpetrators have on at least one occasion made me believe that external entities/spirits/demons had taken over my body," 530 (53%) said "Yes."

7. Novel torture and near-death torture, including anoxia, brachycardia, and cardiac arrest due to suffocation, electrocution, freezing, drowning, etc., to induce tabula rasa programmable states to form. Of 1109 EAS respondents who replied to the item: "Near drowning experience caused by perpetrators," 565 (51%) said "Yes."

8. Torture, especially electroshock, to "anchor" (set deeply) programming in the unconscious mind. Of 1119 EAS respondents who replied to the item: "My memories of extreme abuse include electroshock" 558 (50%) said "Yes."

9. Programming beginning in the first two, three, or four years of life serving as a foundation for later programming. Of 975 EAS respondents who replied to the item: "I was subjected to government-sponsored mind control experimentation at birth through 2 years," 139 (14%) said "Yes."

10. Programming to punish the victim when any self-state threatens to disobey abuser directives, especially to never remember or disclose their abuse, including flooding the victim with anxiety, pain, spinning or drugged sensations, illness, self-harm, and suicidality. Some survivors develop an awareness that these experiences are not their own reactions, but originate in programming. Of 997 EAS respondents who replied to the item: "I have experienced self-destruct programming installed in the event I began to remember the programming", 565 (57%%) said "Yes."

11. Self-states programmed to perform particular roles, such as soldier, courier, assassin, cult leader, etc., and skills, such as speaking a foreign language, flying an aircraft, remote-viewing, and sexual behaviour. On the EAS, 175 respondents reported mind control programming through which they were trained to become assassins and 203 respondents reported mind control programming designed to develop psychic abilities.

12. Self-states programmed as tape-recorders and computers to store information.

13. Self-states programmed to report in to handlers by phone and to assure ongoing abuser-contact.

14. Anti-therapy programming causing victims to feel "stuck", unable to speak, hear, or remain awake, to create chaos, to be

acutely suicidal, and to disbelieve all memories. Of 1097 EAS respondents who replied to the item about having suicidal thoughts immediately before traumatic memories surface, 737 (68%) said "Yes."

15. Programmed stimuli, for example, hand signals, words, telephone rings or tones, that trigger self-states to experience fear or to perform behaviours unbeknown to the host.

16. Programme codes to access self-states, to install, reset or activate programmes, to turn on back-up (fail-safe) programmes, to erase (remove) programmes, to "set off" explosive devices and to release toxins. Of 967 EAS respondents who replied to the item: "One or more of my alters had access codes", 332 (34%) said "Yes."

Clinical observations of mind control phenomena in victims

I have observed the following indicators of torture-based mind control:

1. Clients suddenly switch, in response to internal or external cues, to automaton-like self-states, with stiff posture, glazed-over eyes, inability to hear or respond, then begin to walk or drive to a phone or destination, with full amnesia in the host for the time in that state. Of 963 EAS respondents who replied to the item: "I have (or have had) at least one robot alter", 270 (28%) said "Yes."

2. Four clients reported the identical code to "remove" the same kind of programme, including about ten characters (details omitted for security and confidentiality) with the same prefix or suffix with spelling variations. This code is not in books or on the internet. These people lived in distant regions. I also observed individuals report very slight variations of a code for another kind of programme.

3. Proper removal codes "disappear" a structure; slightly incorrect codes fail. I have witnessed clients experience enormous relief when a proper removal code caused a structure to "vanish".

4. Identical abuser names and titles, not in books or the internet, reported by geographically distant survivors.

5. I have observed injuries, such as large scars, electroshock burns, and dislocated limbs that I believe were not self-inflicted, and that were consistent with reported programming torture.

6. When clients recall and work to resolve torture-based mind control, they regularly experience acute fear, suicidality, urges to self-harm, dizziness, sleepiness, feeling drugged, jerking as if being electro-shocked, urges to stop therapy, and robotic-like statements of "I must have made it all up," or "I want to go home" (meaning to return to the abusers).

7. Strong fear and startle responses to the phone ringing and extreme sensitivity to indoor lights.

8. Great consistency in reports of programming over time. Present recollections match rediscovered journal-writing, art, sand trays, etc., from as many as ten years earlier.

9. Clients experience marked symptom relief as programming is made conscious and resolved.

Historical evidence

In 1953, Allen Dulles, then director of the USA Central Intelligence Agency (CIA), named Dr Sidney Gottlieb to direct the CIA's MKULTRA programme, which included experiments conducted by psychiatrists to create amnesia, new dissociated identities, new memories, and responses to hypnotic access codes. In 1972, then-CIA director Richard Helms and Gottlieb ordered the destruction of all MKULTRA records. A clerical error spared seven boxes, containing 1738 documents, over 17,000 pages. This archive was declassified through a Freedom of Information Act Request in 1977, though the names of most people, universities, and hospitals are redacted. The CIA assigned each document a number preceded by "MORI", for "Management of Officially Released Information", the CIA's automated electronic system at the time of document release. These documents, to be referenced throughout this chapter, are accessible on the Internet (see: http://abuse-of-power.org/modules/content/index.php?id=31). The United States Senate held a hearing exposing the abuses of MKULTRA, entitled "Project MKULTRA, the CIA's program of research into behavioral modification" (1977).

Of 1000 EAS respondents who replied to the item: "Secret government-sponsored mind control experiments were performed on me as a child", 257 (26%) said "Yes," and 219 of those 257 remembered seeing perpetrators wearing white doctors' coats. Of 451 respondents to the Professional Extreme Abuse Survey, seventy-one professional helpers from at least six countries reported work with survivors reporting government mind control experimentation.

Psychological mechanisms underlying programme installation and function

What psychological capacities and mechanisms do programmers manipulate to effect mind control?

The dissociative disorders field has established that DID is associated with chronic, intense, early abuse, often involving a combination of physical, sexual, and emotional abuse, frequently including profound neglect, family violence, and a generally chaotic home environment (Chu, Frey, Ganzel, & Matthews, 1999; Draijer & Langeland, 1999; Ogawa, Sroufe, Weinfield, Carlson, & Egeland, 1997; Putnam, 1997; Pynoos, Steinberg, & Goenjian, 1996; Ross, 1995; van der Kolk, McFarlane, & Weisaeth, 1996). However, responses to acute torture are very different from responses to chronic trauma.

It is also well known that amnestic barriers separate the experience of trauma-bearing self-states, also known as "emotional parts" (EPs), from the awareness of the host (ANP) (Nijenhuis & den Boer, 2007). But how does this inform us on how programmed self-states can effect specific emotional and behavioural responses in the host in mind control victims? Furthermore, what psychological mechanisms allow programmers to "install" directives, codes, structures, harm-producing devices, internal programmers, malevolent entities, and files of information in their victims? How can the mind accurately register such complex information during mental states impeded by torture? How can programming be achieved in the first few years of life? Might torture somehow enhance the mind–brain's capacity to encode information and store it in pristine form?

Incorporating current knowledge on trauma and dissociation, I will explore some of the psychological processes that begin to answer these questions. Some of these mechanisms are well evidenced and some are more theoretical and hypothetical.

Dissociation: use of torture to induce and exploit dissociative processes

A synthesis of survivor accounts suggests that the central psychological mechanism that permits mind control programming to be effected is that extreme torture can force a victim's psyche to form new, readily programmable self-states, separated from the front personality by programmed amnestic barriers, that can be exploited to "hold" and "hide" directives, skills, and information. The conditions that appear to most reliably yield new programmable states are (1) application of torture in the preschool years or to already dissociation-prone individuals, and (2) application of forms of torture that victims have not yet learned to endure, such as novel or extremely prolonged torture.

Some of these self-states are developed into ego states that have the capacity for executive functions, often beginning with the assignment of a name and specific function, followed by extensive conditioning to (1) develop desired skills, (2) learn cues to access and control the ego state, and (3) develop barriers to keep all memory of this abuse from the host. Other induced dissociative states are used for more internal functions, such as holding pain, terror, information, and representations of structures to serve purposes in the inner world.

Is this the stuff of science fiction? Historical and psychological evidence demonstrate otherwise.

USA mind control projects

Declassified CIA documents provide a historical record of MK-ULTRA projects that manipulated amnestic and dissociative states.

MORI 017395 states that Subproject 136 (1961) would use drugs and hypnosis to induce and control dissociative states, including multiple personality disorder, and would use "psychological tricks", reward, punishment, and electroshock to control behaviour, including that of children.

MORI 090527 (1951) http://abuse-of-power.org/modules/content/index.php?id=31http://michael-robinett.com/declass/c000.htm details an experiment that successfully placed two girls in "very deep trance", and used post-hypnotic coded words to make them carry and activate a bomb, followed by instructions for absolute amnesia.

Gresch (personal communication, 2010) reports that he and other children were programmed to be suicide bombers in the 1960s in what was probably a NATO project (including the CIA) to defend West Germany against the Warsaw Pact with tactical nuclear weapons, including portable "Special Atomic Demolition Munitions" (never actually deployed). Gresch reports that the children were programmed to lie in wait in foxholes, ready to detonate these "mini-nukes" against Soviet tanks that were to be manoeuvred into "killing zones".

MORI 190713 (1955), "Hypnotism and Covert Operations", discusses placing the "conscious mind in a state of suspended animation" to make subjects "have amnesia both for the fact of having been hypnotized and the origin of whatever new idea or impetus to action has been implanted in his unconscious mind".

In an article in the *Providence Evening Bulletin* of 13 May 1968, George Estabrook, described as a former consultant for the FBI and CIA, is quoted as stating, "the key to creating an effective spy or assassin rests in splitting a man's personality, or creating multipersonality" (Ross, 2000, p. 162).

Tien

Psychiatrist H. C. Tien developed electrolytic or electricity/love therapy (ELT) in the early 1970s (Tien, 1974). Tien discovered that torture, particularly electroshock, combined with directives, can "erase" a patient's original identity, beliefs, and name, and replace these with an identity, beliefs, and name chosen by the "therapist", congruent with the process of torture-based mind control.

Cameron

In the 1950s, Ewen Cameron, MD, of Allan Memorial Institute at McGill University in Montreal "treated" non-consenting patients, most probably diagnosed with schizophrenia, in what inarguably amounted to torture. Between 1957 and 1960, MKULTRA funded this research (Weinstein, 1988).

Cameron's treatment had two phases. In the "depatterning" phase, for fifteen to thirty days (sixty-five days in some cases), patients were administered massive doses of LSD and electroshock, usually combined with prolonged, drug-induced sleep, to ultimately induce a "tabula rasa" state and "complete amnesia" for one's life (Cleghorn, 1990; Marks, 1979; McGonigle, 1999). The "psychic driving" phase followed, sixteen hours a day for several weeks. Patients were forced to listen to endless loop taped descriptions of their painful past and inadequacies, sometimes accompanied by shocking their legs to intensify the negative effect, followed by, for two to five weeks, listening to tapes describing how they wanted to get well and the behaviours to facilitate this, such as becoming self-assertive (an interesting irony) (Marks, 1979).

Harvey Weinstein (1988), psychiatrist and son of a victim, aptly describes Cameron's work as "a wholesale attempt to erase minds and reprogramme" subjects (p. 147), assisted by MKULTRA.

In both Cameron's "treatment" and in mind control, torture, primarily electroshock, is applied to induce a tabula rasa state, followed by attempts to develop a brand-new persona.

Use of electricity to modify soldiers' behaviour in the First World War

Electroshock was used by military psychiatry to eradicate unwanted behaviour in soldiers since at least the First World War. The goal was to override soldiers' "weakness", such as "hysterical pseudo-paralysis", to get them back to the front (Fassin, Rechtman, & Gomme). Noteworthy were French neurologist, Clovis Vincent, who "boasted of regularly obtaining rapid results after what he termed a 'merciless struggle' between the patient and doctor" (ibid., p. 48), and German physician Fritz Kaufmann; his "Kaufmann cure" involved application of powerful alternating currents to paralysed limbs (Rejali, 2009, p. 136).

Austrian psychiatrist Wilhelm Neutra (1920), treated soldiers with "fiercely painful faradic [electric] currents" in 1914, and claimed that over 100 psychiatrists applied these methods since the beginning of the Great War.

Neutra reasoned that war hysteria is a subconscious conflict between the instinct of self-preservation and patriotism or morale. He believed that if hysterical behaviour becomes associated with pain produced by the electroshock, the subconscious is going to search for a better solution.

The same basic psychological mechanism is used in much mind control. The dissociated fear of torture is greater than the fear of executing the self-endangering behaviour desired by the programmer.

Although we may never have evidence of torture-based mind control directly evolving from military electroshock treatments, I believe the likelihood is high.

Pavlov

Ivan Pavlov is most famous for his discovery of classical conditioning based on research with dogs. Pavlov presented a warning signal (the conditioned stimulus), such as a bell, and shortly after (e.g., five seconds), gave the dogs an unconditioned stimulus (such as food). The warning signal then produces a conditioned reflex, such as "food excitation" (e.g., salivation).

Lesser-known is that Pavlov also used electroshock as a warning stimulus. We now understand this as a form of fear conditioning, the basis for kinds of mind control that rely on victim responses of fear and pain to programmed external and internal cues (discussed later).

Still less known is that Pavlov also studied the effects of overwhelming stress on the dogs' prior conditioning (Pavlov, 1941; Sargant, 1957).

In the Leningrad flood of 1924, water seeped under the laboratory door and Pavlov's dogs nearly drowned, swimming in "terror with heads at the tops of their cages" (Sargant, 1957, p. 17). Many lost all prior conditioning. Pavlov described the dogs as dissociating cortical and subcortical mental activity, and being in a state of hypnosis, similar to some human "mental disease". Pavlov surmised that in severe trauma, "the brain might be wiped almost clean, at least temporarily, of all the conditioned behavior patterns recently implanted in it" (Sargant, 1957, pp. 16–17). With months of patient work, Pavlov reconditioned most dogs. Then he let a trickle of water run under the laboratory door and the dogs all panicked and were re-traumatized, again losing all prior learning.

Pavlov's observations parallel survivors' reports of tabula rasa states forming in mind-control torture: all prior learning is lost, "wiped clean", and a trauma trigger reactivates the trauma state.

Sargant

British psychiatrist William Sargant is probably best known for his work on "acute war neurosis" ("battle fatigue", "shell shock") with Second World War soldiers (1957). In addition, he directly studied the effects of overwhelming stress on humans, as Pavlov did with dogs.

Sargant compared "war neuroses" to Pavlov's "experimental neuroses" in dogs. He observed stress-induced "states of greatly increased suggestibility" in combat soldiers (*ibid.*, pp. 24–46), as well as in people who had undergone prolonged emotional and physiological stress in sudden religious conversion and political/ideological brainwashing.

Sargant claimed that the immediate effect of severe stress in humans and animals is "usually to impair judgement and increase suggestibility" (*ibid.*, p. 82). He imposed severe stress on patients so that "some of the new abnormal patterns may disperse, and the healthier ones can return or be implanted afresh in the brain", much like Cameron. Sargant also applied similar stressors, including states of fear and anger, insulin shock, electroshock, and prolonged drug-induced sleep, up to fourteen or fifteen days, in a "sleep treatment ward" (Freeman, 1987).

Sargant and Cameron both had espionage ties, Sargant to British Secret Intelligence (Sargant, 1957), Cameron to the CIA (Thomas, 1989, p. 208, 1998). Sargant and Cameron had met several times

(Thomas, 1998) and may have been friends (Collins, 1988, p. 42). Sargant had also met with Gottlieb, director of MKULTRA (Thomas, 1998).

Snapping and cult indoctrination as dissociative processes

Conway and Siegelman, in *Snapping: America's Epidemic of Sudden Personality Change* (2005) explain that ceremonial rituals for cult indoctrination, including repetitive chanting, meditation, suggestion, sometimes food and sleep deprivation and infliction of pain, finally result in a "snap":

> an experience that is unmistakably traumatic . . . Sudden change comes in a moment of intense experience . . . an unforeseen break in the continuity of awareness that may leave them detached, withdrawn, disoriented—and utterly confused. The experience itself may produce hallucinations or delusions or render the person extremely vulnerable to suggestion . . . [p. 5]

This experience conforms to mind control survivor reports that extreme abuse, isolation, sleep and food deprivation, sensory and ideological bombardment, and fear-inducing illusions, suddenly induce the formation of a suggestible mental state that are receptive to new ideologies.

The ancient Greek initiation ritual into the "Greater Mysteries" incorporated elements of sentencing the initiate to death, amnesia-producing drugs, rebirth, and renaming to erase prior memory and induce receptiveness to the formation of a new identity (Graves, in Sargant, 1957, pp. 194–195).

Ritual abuse survivors describe the same steps in rebirth, initiation, and marriage rituals: terror, pain, helplessness, and fear of demonic forces, followed by methods to induce amnesia, including drugs, followed by "rebirth" as a member of the group, provision of a new name, a ceremony to marry the "convert" to the group's deity, and a formal claim or announcement of belonging to the group.

Historical accounts of cult indoctrination, Tien, Cameron, Pavlov, Sargant, and First World War electroshock "treatment" of soldiers, and MKULTRA documents citing knowledge of inducing and manipulating amnestic and dissociative states, all support survivor accounts of overwhelming stress inducing the sudden formation of suggestible mental states. Our current knowledge of dissociative processes helps to tie this all together.

Torture in early childhood to induce a dissociation-prone psyche

Torture-based mind control, by most survivor reports, begins before four years of age, usually by age two, to make the psyche dissociation-prone and to serve as a foundation for later programming.

Young children have a greater capacity to enter trance states than older children and adults, allowing for dissociative, self-hypnotic responses to overwhelming stimuli (Putnam, 1997). Peterson (1991) explains,

> Developmentally natural dissociative activities in tandem with primitive defense mechanisms may lead a child to block off painful memories using a dissociative process ... Without a person' conscious volition, a pattern of protective dissociations may begin to develop, creating newly established and increasingly distinct parts of self, encapsulated in time, and memory segments that are unavailable to the rest of that person's consciousness. [p. 153]

Fotheringham (2008) explains that a "pattern of protective dissociations" was natural for her:

> "I," the primary person ... was not aware of these alternate identities or their pieces of "my" life. It seemed natural for life to be broken into chunks ... so "lost time" went unnoticed. Since continuity was unknown, there was no sense of discontinuity ... my brain's way of coping with difficulties was "wired in"—simply create another alter! [p. 499]

Putnam (1997) views DID as a developmental failure to integrate the discrete, state-dependent, aspects of self that are normal in young children into a cohesive sense of self. Support for this view is found in Blinder's (2007) review of the research and neurobiology on the development of an autobiographical self. Blinder concludes that prior to four years of age, a child's sense of self is more disjointed than cohesive, and that an autobiographical self emerges at around four years of age as a function of the child's "ability to hold in mind multiple representations of the world simultaneously".

Gresch believes that programmers understand that the personality lacks cohesion in early childhood, and that they begin abusing victims very early, "to hamper any real personality development to replace it with a subhuman structure, to be used like a programmable robot" (personal communication, 2009).

After the fourth birthday, a relatively coherent sense of self helps protect against formation of fully separate self-states.

Once a "pattern of protective dissociations" has developed, programmers can use torture to induce new dissociative self-states to form, then "build" the behavioural repertoire of these self-states through conditioning, training, hypnotic suggestion, etc. Dissociation-proneness keeps these self-states maximally segregated from each other. Even in adolescence and adulthood, new self-states can be induced to form in dissociation-prone individuals, a capacity exploited by programmers.

Dissociative responses to chronic and acute trauma

What allows suggestible, malleable, self-states to form in response to severe stress? Much of this can be understood by distinguishing the nature of dissociative responses to chronic, lower-intensity trauma from responses to acute, higher-intensity trauma.

In response to chronic, lower-intensity trauma and shame-evoking trauma, self-states are likely to form and remain dissociated largely as a function of an active mental effort of the relatively non-traumatized self to shield itself from awareness of painful or unacceptable memories, thoughts, feelings and motives.

This is the mechanism of self-state formation emphasized by Dell (2009). Dell contends that dissociated self-states are formed by "dissociation-potentiated repression", the defensive use of repression in individuals with substantial self-hypnotic or dissociative ability.

Thus, such dissociative self-states are born, in large part, by an act of self-agency, are more cortical than subcortical, and have the active organizing purpose of coping with the trauma that precipitated their formation. These trauma-bearing self-states are also likely to remain dissociated from the relatively non-traumatized self by way of an ongoing mental defensive effort to disown the unacceptable. Some of these self-states "hold" knowledge of trauma that is intolerable to the host. Some are skilled at managing physical pain. Some may defensively identify with abusers and reject the self. Some may be internal self-helpers (ISHs).

Having formed to protect the self, I believe that these ego states are somewhat less susceptible to mind control, and, in some cases, successfully elude detection by the abusers.

In contrast, in response to acute and higher-intensity trauma, the victim is likely to react more reflexively and instinctually. These responses probably largely derive from subcortical mechanisms that activate very quickly in response to perceived threat to physical or psychic survival, vs. purposeful, slower, cortically mediated mental activity (LeDoux, 1996). Some of these responses involve hyper-arousal, including fight/rage, flight/panic, and sympathetic nervous system arousal. Some involve hypo-arousal, including immobilization/freezing, passive submission, numbing, derealization, depersonalization, impaired attention and cognition, and lowered heart rate, breath rate, and muscle tone. These states are more a function of intense emotional and physiological states taking precedence over cognitive coping strategies as the trauma occurs, than the psyche's efforts to extrude intolerable knowledge from awareness (van der Kolk, McFarlane, & Weisaeth, 1996).

A third response to high-intensity trauma, perhaps only a reaction to perceived immediate threat to life, combines elements of hypo- and hyper-arousal. This state is characterized by sudden and surprising calm, absence of fear or pain regardless of the extent of injury, intensely focused attention, sensory hyper-acuity, mental quickness, and an expanded sense of time (Dell, 2009; Heim, 1892).

Mind control survivors report that self-states formed in response to high-intensity trauma arise spontaneously due to a break in self-agency, and are mentally registered apart from the other self-states from their inception. Accordingly, they remain dissociated from the host with less mental effort than self-states formed defensively. They intently focus on accommodating their abusers. Some remain internally "fixed in space and time", reliving the pain and terror that provoked their formation (van der Hart, Nijenhuis, & Steele, 2006). Some perceive the pain and terror of the trauma they endured as "normal", the only reality they know.

The model of "structural dissociation of the personality" of Steele, van der Hart, and Nijenhuis (2009) is close to what I believe occurs when self-states form in response to high-intensity, acute trauma, such as torture. Their model emphasizes that traumatic material is registered differently and apart from benign experience, as it occurs. They contend that an ongoing integrative deficit results in a structural dissociation of the personality, and only secondarily is this division a result of a psychological defence. They posit that when individuals experience aversive stimuli, such as a major threat, mental and behavioural "action tendencies" are activated to avoid or escape the threat. Such experience is registered in "emotional parts" of the personality, a separate psychobiological system than that employed to approach attractive stimuli and adapt to daily life, the "apparently normal parts of the personality". If overwhelming trauma occurs to a child, or if a primary attachment figure is frightening, this hinders the otherwise normal developmental progression towards integration of the two psychobiological systems. The host's phobic avoidance of traumatic memory held in emotional parts maintains the division, which probably involves a preconscious mental effort, a psychological defence.

States formed in response to high-intensity trauma are more rudimentary than self-states formed with less intense trauma. Some have a limited sense of "me-ness". Many are only "fragments". Both can develop an increased sense of self over time. For example, self-states formed in response to a particular kind of abuse tend to take executive control whenever that abuse is reapplied, and can have an autobiographical self within those episodes, including experiencing themselves as the age of the body at the last episode of that abuse.

Programmers use rudimentary self-states to construct personae to perform desired functions. Gresch (personal communication, 2008) explains that a young child's immediate response to torture is to enter a survival-driven state of hypnotic heightened attentiveness and suggestibility that is ultra-receptive to learning. Thus primed, this state may be exploited in limited ways, such as "fragments" trained to obey commands or perform circumscribed behaviours to avoid punishment. Or, this state may be further augmented through a long-term "torture-hypno-conditioning process", to carry out more complex executive functions. Terror controls this type of self-state long-term, in that it is stuck, "unable to leave the torture chamber in its own mind".

In many cases, survivors discover self-states that appear motivated to serve their own needs, to later discover that programmers deliberately orchestrated their organizing purpose. For example, some ego-states see themselves as powerful or believe themselves to be "chosen" for some honoured position, but they are amnestic for the early, severe abuse, that forced their formation and kept them controlled. Genuinely human needs motivate such parts, but they are not born of psychological defence; they are deliberately induced to form, then conditioned and manipulated.

I believe that practitioners of torture-based mind control have a depth understanding of all of these kinds of dissociative states, calculatingly induce some types to form, limit some to holding pain and terror, condition some to perform executive functions of more complexity, manipulate "self-created" ego states to the degree that they can, all to exploit the unique properties of each to the fullest.

Torture to induce formation of self-states

Mind control survivors report that their abusers understand well that torture induces a dissociation-prone psyche to form new programmable self-states, and calculatedly torture victims for this purpose.

Carol Rutz, mind control survivor and author of *A Nation Betrayed* (2001), believes that existing self-states tend to "come up" in sequence from older to younger, to distribute the burden of torture being applied, until finally a defenceless baby appears, less capable of using the mind to cope, and more programmable (personal communication, 2009).

Many survivors claim that sophisticated abusers recognize that a new self-state has arisen when the child no longer reacts with terror or pain to the torture. This new state is immediately named and given directives. Abusers may also "install" the perception of entities and structures. These messages, entities, and structures become paired with pain and terror in the new trauma-bound state, which has no cognitive capacity to process or reject any of this input. This all remains dissociated from the host.

In this vignette, Rutz and her two-year-old self-state, "Little Girl", recount programming at age four, designed to form a new self-state, "Samantha". After administering a "truth drug", the doctor says:

"Come forth little one—I need to know your name!"

"Little girl."

Then the doctor says, "Who else?"

"Nobody."

He knows we's lyin so he makes our body jump and hurt real bad. We got lectricity going through us.

"Shadow, our name is shadow."

Now they want to know who Shadow is.

Shadow gotted made at Grandfathers' before we came here [describes ritual that induced the formation of Shadow].

Now they knows all our names. If ya knows our names—ya got power and control. They says theys gonna give us special numbers. Later Dr No, the lady Doctor says, "We are gonna help you, little girl, not to have any more pain. You don't have to feel it ever again."

"They's gonna make Samantha come . . ."

(Intense electro-shock was delivered in order to allow my mind to dissociate and create Samantha who would never feel pain. In the future, whenever I was put through a tortuous painful experience, Samantha would automatically be the alter who took over the body and she would hide the memory and the pain from the rest of the system . . .).

"Back, just let the memories go back"

That be what the doctor tellin us alright. [Rutz, 2001, pp. 17–18]

In 2009, I asked Carol Rutz to help me understand how Samantha could both "never feel pain", yet "hide the memory and pain from the rest of the system". She explained,

> "Samantha" took the pain and hid it from the rest of the system. So she really did feel pain, even though the lie [by the abusers] was that she would not. So, she "complied" and consciously believed she did not feel pain, but she did hold the pain, less consciously. The rest of the system did not feel pain. "Little Girl" certainly believed Samantha did not feel pain, and that was important because she was one of the main presenting alters. Whenever a situation occurred where pain was administered the alter, Samantha came out and encapsulated the pain.

"Blank slate" programmable mental states

Many survivors report that in response to prolonged, especially novel, torture, victims suddenly stop resisting and enter a paradoxically calm, pain-free, highly receptive and programmable mental state. They describe a psychophysiological mental state, not a state with a sense of identity. An anonymous survivor (2008) described this as "kind of like a memory stick for a computer. Not a fragment—just an object waiting to be written on."

Fotheringham (2008) explains that novel torture reliably elicits such states:

> Do a new form of torture. If it is a familiar form of torture, it will just default to the one who is programmed to take that . . . A new part forms . . . totally linked to self-defense and self-protection . . . constantly looking outward to know what to do to stay safe . . .

Gresch (personal communication, 2008) describes this process:

> To evoke a "blank slate", the torture must proceed until the victim stops resisting, beyond any feigned compliance, beyond the point of genuine obedience and submission, until the victim finally surrenders all personal intention, and then the programmers push even further, and achieve their goal, the blank slate state . . . The victim is calm and receptive. This is the physiological reaction to torture if applied in the right way . . . Your last chance for survival

depends on receptiveness to everything the situation commands of you ... The victim reaches a state in which it is extremely suggestible, in an extremely hypnotic state, ready to accept everything ... They can implant a so-called "personality", actually a script of personality, in this highly receptive ultra-learning state.

Gresch explained (personal communication, 2009) how this newly formed state does not experience pain or terror, yet is ultimately controlled by pain and terror in the moment and long-term:

This new state does not register in consciousness the painful torture that precipitated its formation, yet less conscious pain and terror continually fuel its receptivity and hyper-attention. Though dissociated states segregate this experience as it occurs, it is registered to some degree as a whole in the mind/brain. The programmed information is preserved intact, with little deterioration over time, largely through an associational neural network connecting it to the preceding pain and terror.

Dell (2009), in a recent synopsis of the literature on "peritraumatic dissociation", provides support for survivor accounts of tabula rasa states forming in response to life-threatening trauma. He explains that in response to perceived threat to life, people automatically enter a state of "absence of pain, absence of fear, a calm state of mind, a slowing of time, accelerated thought, clear thinking, heightened sensory perception, and a heightened ability to execute motor skills with precision and confidence" (p. 762). Dell describes this response as "situation-specific", "task-oriented", and lasting "only as long as that life-threatening situation lasts" (p. 761). He calls this "evolution-prepared dissociation", in that "perception is immediately adjusted and instantly tuned to the most survival-relevant aspects of the environment" (p. 760). Such a mental state would make torture victims highly receptive to programming.

Support for this phenomenon is found in the work of Albert Heim, who documented the experience of survivors of near-fatal falls in 1892. Heim found that 95% of fall victims experienced a mental state of "heightened sensory and ideational activity, and without anxiety or pain" (p. 135), the same mental state described by torture-based mind control survivors. Heim said of his own near-fatal fall, "my thoughts and ideas were coherent and very clear, and in no way susceptible, as are dreams, to obliteration" (p. 134). Heim noted that hearing was the last sense to be lost. The ability to hear in near-death situations and enhanced memory acuity would both facilitate the objectives of mind control.

Psychological impact of naming new self-states

Assignment of names to self-states is central to mind control, as it was to Tien's electrolytic love therapy. Abusers quickly assign names to define new self-states, such as "Evil", or "Lolita". Self-states tend to perceive themselves as belonging to whomever named them. If the programmer delays in assigning a name, and the self-state can name, it may be able to elude the trainer. Names allow programmers to call self-states forward. Survivors often guard the names of self-states to prevent their being summoned.

Gresch (personal communication, 2009) explains, "The art of mind control is the art of controlling attention". Names are a means for programmers to manipulate this attention. He explains,

> Names combined with code phrases trigger the execution of programmed mental mechanisms, that is, thoughts, emotion, and behavior, in compliance with programmer instructions, fueled by fear conditioning. For example, if somebody says "I am your god, Peter Munk, one two three", a programmed self-state based on a modified prototype of "Peter Munk," a character in Wilhelm Hauff's fairy tale, "Das kalte Herz," [1858] will be activated. Peter Munk is unemotional, obedient, lacking in self-awareness, and motivated to avoid torture. This alter has been torture-hypno-conditioned to execute a number of mental actions, including (1) to activate Hugo, an other alter, to take the pain if Munk is tortured, (2) to report any access to the programmer, and (3) should any intention to resist programming enter the conscious mind, the image of a "pillar of power" will appear, the words will be heard in a threatening manner in the inner ear, the mind will be flooded with depression, and the conscious mind will feel a compulsion to once again be obedient to relieve the depression.

Gresch explained how this programming involving the "pillar of power" was effected:

The "pillar of power" was a magical object in the inner world of the "alter", Peter Munk, which symbolized the concentrated power of the perpetrators. Peter Munk was instructed to imagine the pillar of power with his inner eye. He was then told to image that he was trying to pass the pillar of power, and to give a sign with his hand when he was about to do this. When he gave the sign, he was electro-shocked through an electrode fastened to his penis. The programmer commanded, "You shouldn't try to betray me. Look! I now allow you to recognize that we have attached measuring sensors to your head. We have recorded the brain waves when you are trying to pass the pillar of power. We know what you are doing". It doesn't matter whether the perpetrators really were able to manage this. What counts was that Peter Munk believed it.

Polyvagal theory

What neurobiological mechanisms account for the formation of highly programmable self-states and mental states in response to torture? Stephen Porges' *Polyvagal Theory* (1995, 1999) provides some clues.

The vagus nerve is the longest of ten cranial nerves and is critical in responding to threat. Porges specifies two distinct branches of the vagus nerve in mammals: (1) The *smart vagus*, the phylogenetically newer, ventral branch, and (2) The *vegetative vagus*, the phylogenetically older, dorsal branch.

In response to threat, the smart (ventral) vagus first deploys the parasympathetic nervous system (PNS), activates socially affiliative behaviour with the same species, that is, help-seeking, and maintains relative calm. If this cannot effectively manage the threat, it shifts its strategy to fight or flight, mediated by the sympathetic nervous system (SNS). If fight or flight cannot adequately cope with the stressor, the vegetative (dorsal) vagus activates, inhibiting the heart via the PNS, yielding a "shut-down" of behaviour, tonic immobility, freezing, death-feigning, or submission to the threat. This reptilian/amphibian response may be considered a dissociative response (Beauchaine, Gatzke-Kopp, & Mead, 2007), perhaps similar to "evolution-prepared dissociation" as described by Dell (2009).

I corresponded with Porges in 2008 to determine whether the dorsal vagal responses of submission or paralysis may relate to mental states induced to form under torture, and whether such states might be receptive to encoding information, that is, being programmed. Porges explained that "a physiological state, in part, mediated by the dorsal vagal complex might promote dissociative states". Porges also said that he believes that dorsal vagal states are mediated, in part, by oxytocin, a hormone important in pair bonding and social memory, and that this might yield strong bonds to the perpetrator (an other critical element in programming). He said that dorsal vagal states might facilitate one-trial learning, a rapid, relatively indelible conditioned response, closely connected to fear conditioning. He said that learning in this dorsal vagal state "may be disconnected from the experience and this may form the basis of a different personality structure". He was careful to add that these hypotheses, and how they relate to states of calmness, remain to be tested.

Thus, the dorsal vagal threat response may contribute to a calm, receptive state, perhaps similar to Dell's "evolution-prepared dissociation" (2009), that may be highly receptive to encoding information via one-trial learning and to bonding to the abuser, and information encoded in such states may become stored in a "different personality structure", all responses advantageous for mind control.

Introjection of abusers and programmers

Most clinicians in the dissociative disorders field agree that internal representations of abusers are commonplace in DID, and that these are usually self-states who have taken on the demeanour of frightening abusers. Psychological mechanisms that drive the formation of "abuser self-states" include many variants of identification with the aggressor. Their "masks" often conceal young, trauma-bearing states. Many mind control survivors also report discovering self-states who were programmed to take on abuser characteristics in order to control other self-states.

Many survivors also perceive within them internalized programmers, witchcraft spirits, and entities that are not self-states at all. These are experienced as "foreign bodies" installed in mind control.

I believe that programmers often intentionally "install" representations of themselves in mind-control torture. Gresch (personal communication, 2009) explains,

> The victim must execute the orders of the programmers when they are not present. So they try to "implant" themselves into the mind of the victim ... Through torture, the perpetrators switch off the critical mind of the victim ... All of the torture-enhanced faculties are exclusively fixed to the commands of the programmer, just like in hypnosis. This is much more than obeying—it is introjecting the perpetrators ... The generic abuser maltreats the victim to satisfy his needs. But the mind controller uses torture and pain to transform the psyche of the victim.

Above, Carol Rutz described the torture-driven formation of "Samantha". The next day, Rutz explains that, using drugs and hypnosis, Gottlieb created twin self-states specifically for government mind control: "Baby", who was told it lived in "Neverland", and "Guy" to live in "Shadowland" (Rutz, personal communication, 2009). Then Gottlieb commanded, "The genie appears when Neverland is opened. Remember, I am your master and I am the genie" (Rutz, 2001, p. 19). Although survival-driven attachment needs are at play here, I believe that the internalization of this Gottlieb–genie must be understood as a foreign body, a psychological introject, not a self-state.

Many survivors also describe rituals in which witchcraft abusers "placed" parts of their "spirits" inside of them, usually in specific self-states, through the transfer of body fluids and substances. "Attached spirits" are perceived to internally repeat the controlling messages first spoken in rituals, such as, "You belong to me", "You will obey me", etc. Commonly, such abusers also "attach" their deities to strengthen the spirits' effects. Affected self-states may also perceive that the abusers captured parts of their own spirit to hold captive within themselves.

Even if the host views such "transfers" as impossible, self-states formed and indoctrinated in the "theology" of these abusers generally perceive them as very real, and the impact is devastating, as they feel inhabited by these "attached" entities.

Programming the unconscious mind

Many survivors report that programmers ultimately seek to install mind control beneath the level of all self-states in what their programmers called the "unconscious mind".

The CIA document MORI 190713, "Hypnotism and covert operations" (1955) explains that an "operator" can use hypnosis to place the "conscious mind" in a state of "suspended animation" to "reach and affect the unconscious mind directly", to "successfully" "transplant ideas and motives", that are felt to be one's "own free will", with post-hypnotic amnesia for the hypnosis. This document explains the powerful compulsion to follow hypnotically placed dictates:

> Let us suppose that a good hypnotic subject has entered the deepest stage of hypnosis. If the operator then suggests, "After I awaken you, you will have no recollection of what has occurred. Furthermore, exactly 1 hour after you are awakened you will go to the nearest telephone and dial (any number). To whomever answers you will say (any message)," in all likelihood the subject will do just that ... If the subject after awakening remembers or is *told* that he has been given a post-hypnotic suggestion, what it is, and when it will become operative, he still will experience the greatest difficulty in resisting it. Almost the only way in which he can obtain release from an almost intolerable feeling of discomfort is to carry out the post-hypnotic suggestion as given him; or, alternatively, have the suggestion removed under hypnosis. For what has been created is very similar to, if not identical with a compulsion neurosis. [*ibid.*, p. 8]

Survivors report that the unconscious mind is accessed in lengthy near-death torture by a complete breach of self-agency after all self-states have been taxed beyond endurance, before the victim can create another self-state, before the victim loses physical consciousness, or occasionally in the moments between two pre-existing states taking executive control. One psychologist-survivor explained (2009): "When you have an alter, you are fortified. You are motivated to protect the self. The space in between alters is when they can get to the unconscious mind."

Survivors report that, once accessed, the mind is "laid bare" and records information with no ability to process, question, or reject input. It has no self-awareness, no emotion, no ability to act on its own behalf. It "believes", or, more accurately, "takes in whole", what it is told or shown. This is when programmers reportedly "install" much foundational programming, especially structures to organize the system of self-states.

Survivors report that structures are installed using commands and illusions. A child, having previously been shown a model of a building, may be told, "The building we showed you is in your mind". The programmer may project a grid on a child's chest, then command, "The grid is in your chest", "Go inside the grid". The programmer might put a button on a child's navel and command that the button detonates a bomb if the child ever remembers. These commands and illusions become paired with the torture applied immediately before and after. Steve Oglevie, mind control consultant (personal communication, 1996 to 2006), explains that this causes the structures, illusions, and commands to be perceived to be as real as the torture itself. Schwartz (2000), in a chapter largely devoted to mind control in his book, *Dialogues with Forgotten Voices*, explains:

> [T]he power of all statements made during and immediately after abusive episodes while the victim is in an altered state will be enhanced by the absence of an operative critical consciousness (Conway, 1994) and by the indelible connection with intense fear, intolerable anxiety, or mind-shattering dread. [p. 318]

Because programming "installed" in the unconscious mind was never consciously registered in any self-state, it is usually more "deeply buried".

Blank-slate mental states and the "unconscious mind" are similar, but not identical. Victims report that programmers use the unconscious mind as a writable memory chip to store information, and use blank-slate mental states to develop self-states that can take executive control to serve abuser functions.

Massive memory storage

MKULTRA was interested in the use of hypnosis for enhanced memory storage and retrieval. MORI 190713 (1955) states:

Post-hypnotic suggestions . . . have been known to endure for years. The image that comes to mind is a blackboard on which a message will endure until erased or blurred by time. [p. 9]

. . . a hypnotized person can recall past events with astonishing clarity and detail, in many cases when he does not realize with his conscious mind that he "remembers". [p. 19]

. . . One's memory for detail under such conditions appears to be boundless. [p. 21]

Enhanced memory capacity is critical to much mind control, including memory for lengthy codes, secret information storage, enhanced skills, etc. Can human memory be enhanced to this degree?

Many survivors report that intelligent infants are selected for mind control programmes. And many survivors report having eidetic recall.

Many survivors also report training for acute memory and sensory skills, including being punished, often with electroshock, for failing to remember, failing to discriminate between similar stimuli, and failing to perceive low-grade stimuli. MORI 017395 (1961) http://abuse-of-power.org/modules/content/index.php?id=31http://michael-robinett.com/declass/c000.htm states,

Learning studies will be instituted in which the subject will be rewarded or punished for his overall performance and reinforced in various ways - by being told whether he was right, by being told what the target was, with electroshock etc. [p. 6]

Gresch (personal communication, 2009) explains,

Like many victims, I was "programmed" with the tape recorder metaphor. I was trained to remember complex semantic information . . . If I failed, I was tortured . . . Application of torture causes the programmed information, programmed "post-hypnotic" cues to retrieve the information, and the pain and terror of the torture to be paired together and subconsciously isolated in ultra-long-term memory.

The capacity of the mind for vast information storage is supported by cases of hypermnesia and "hyperthymestic syndrome" (Parker, Cahill, & McGaugh, 2006; Tammet, 2007).

I believe that programmers have learned to combine torture-based conditioning and the use of high-intellect victims to access and exploit a capacity for hypermnesia that may exist in many people.

Programming the host

Survivors report that extensive programming is done to develop a front/host personality who behaves "normally" and is amnestic for the abuse and the existence of programmed self-states.

In "successful" programming, the host is shell-like, lacking much sense of self. It functions like a chameleon, adapting to the demands of each setting. Clinically, it suffers alexithymia, derealization, and depersonalization.

Survivors with shell-like hosts may be more likely to have had foundational programming in infancy. This often includes a division in the psyche between (1) the "normal" side, amnestic for the abuse, often associated with the daytime and right side of the body, and (2) the side entrenched in the abuse, often associated with the night-time and the left side of the body.

In some survivors, the host has some substance, depth, and emotional range. It is more of an agent of self motivated by genuine needs, curiosity, etc. In this case, dissociative barriers between the host and programmed parts may have formed largely through defensive processes, rather than exclusively by programmer design. Although such hosts are usually initially amnestic for their torture and relatively traumatophobic, they are usually more motivated to approach trauma material than shell-like hosts.

The interface of programmed self-states and the host

Two main mechanisms appear to control the interface between programmed self-states and the host: (1) specialized programmed self-states control "switching" of executive control between programmed self-states and the host, and (2) the pain and terror of programmed self-states flood the personality system when the host or other self-states violate programming (see next section).

Pierre Janet's famous case of Lucie illustrates this first mechanism. Janet hypnotized Lucie to carry out post-hypnotic suggestions. Lucie executed these, but forgot doing so immediately afterwards. Lucie was also amnestic for being hypnotized. In contrast, Adrienne, Lucie's second "hypnotic personality", recalled everything that happened while Lucie was hypnotized, and claimed that she executed the post-hypnotic suggestions without Lucie's knowledge (Dell, 2009, pp. 715–716).

In successful mind-control, the host functions much like Lucie. The host is unaware of programmed parts or the directives they execute, but key programmed parts are aware of the host and largely control it, as did Adrienne.

Gresch (personal communication, 2009) explains that his controllers relied on three mechanisms: (1) a front façade, unaware of the abuse and other self-states, (2) a system of obedient robotic self-states, and (3) isolation of the "kernel", the essence of his original self, which the programmers knew they could not extinguish, so must isolate. Obedience by all self-states was ensured by Peter Munk, "the mediator", who believed that his controllers monitored his brain waves and would detect any intention to disobey. If resistance to any directive entered consciousness, programmed parts would re-experience their torture, pain would flood into consciousness, and the "front" would feel compelled to perform as directed.

Unconscious implicit memory for trauma and fear conditioning

Torture-based mind control relies on the capacity to induce victims to re-experience their torture should they violate programme directives, while ensuring that the host remains amnestic for the source of his/her distress. Well-established psychological mechanisms explain how this "works".

LeDoux (1996, 2007) provides extensive neurological and psychological evidence for two long-term memory systems: (1) an explicit memory system that is more conscious, cognitive, and verbal, and (2) an implicit memory system that is more unconscious, emotional, and non-verbal. LeDoux's research reveals that implicit, unconscious memory of pain and fear "may represent an indelible form of learning" (p. 204). In post-trauma responses, "stimuli associated with the danger or trauma become *learned triggers* that unleash emotional reactions in us" (LeDoux, 1996, p. 150). LeDoux calls this form of classical conditioning "fear conditioning".

Fear conditioning appears to be fundamental to how torture-based mind control "works".

LeDoux's research shows that emotional information is largely subcortically mediated by the amygdala in responses engineered for survival—fast, largely automatic, and unconscious. In contrast, cortical responding is slower, conscious, and allows for mental flexibility, decision-making, and execution of one's will in choosing how to respond.

LeDoux (1996) explains that much emotional learning, especially fear conditioning, "operates independently of consciousness—it is part of what we called the emotional unconscious" (p. 128). The largely unconscious "emotional system" more strongly affects the conscious cognitive system than vice versa. Thus, "people normally do all sorts of things for reasons they are not consciously aware of (because the behavior is produced by brain systems that operate unconsciously)" (p. 33); ". . . we are often in the dark about why we feel the way we do" (pp. 52–53).

Survivors report that programmers intentionally use torture and drugs to attempt to block victims' capacity for conscious cognitive processing. They then fear-condition trauma-bound self-states. Then, fear-conditioned responses are automatically executed outside of conscious, cognitive awareness.

Van der Hart, Nijenhuis, and Steele's (2006) theory of structural dissociation dovetails neatly with LeDoux's model of fear conditioning. In their model, EPs have a very limited sense of self, largely restricted to re-experiencing trauma. They store amygdala-mediated emotional and sensorimotor memories of terror and perceived threat, and are often fixated in past trauma with little awareness of passage of time.

Both models help us understand torture-based mind control, which relies on storage of memory for noxious emotional and somatic states in the subconscious implicit memory system of trauma-bearing EPs, and leakage of these implicit memories into the consciously experienced emotions, sensations, thoughts, impulses, and behaviours of ANP(s). When programming is working "well", ANPs remain "in the dark" about the derivation of these noxious responses in the torture-conditioning of EPs.

Conditioned "triggers", such as an abuser's voice, hand signals, etc., induce uncontrolled fear and pain in the ANP. Similarly, failure to perform in ways that avoided pain and terror by the EP, such as compliance with directives, induces a powerful need in the ANP to perform the conditioned behaviour.

It is clearly advantageous for programmers to "place" fear-driven programming in the largely unconscious amygdala and to bypass the conscious, will-based cortex. Accordingly, programmers maximally fear-condition the amygdala-bound implicit memory system, largely within trauma-bearing EPs, to induce automatic responding, and maximally block cortical cognitive processing to attempt to eradicate critical thinking and assertion of free will.

Operant conditioning

Operant conditioning, that is, the use of reward and punishment to increase or decrease behaviours, is a mainstay of mind-control torture, usually applied to condition the behaviour of specific self-states.

In this example of programming of almost unfathomable cruelty, Gresch (personal communication, 2008) provides an example of punishment with a twist—by proxy. Another victim is killed to train his "mediator" personality to properly allocate memories, to remember what the abusers want him to remember and to forget what they want him to forget:

> The flower game: Forget me and forget-me-not: A perpetrator confronts the child with a list of common words like cow, flower, chair, or so. Every word is connected with "forget me" or "forget-me-not". The list becomes longer and longer. The child is punished if he/she remembers or forgets the wrong words. Then the day of the big test comes. Target child is not tested, but another, expendable child. The test is staged as a ritual, maybe a Satanic ritual. When the tested child makes a mistake, the master of ceremonies kills this expendable child with a knife in front of the eyes of the target child.

Drug effects

MKULTRA drug experimentation on unwitting subjects is extensively documented (Ross, 2000; Scheflin & Opton, 1978; Thomas, 1989; Weinstein, 1988) including extensive evidence of testing drug effects on suggestibility, hypnotic states, psychophysiological stress responses, amnesia, and as truth serums for interrogation (e.g., MORI 017441, 144686, 190713).

Mind control survivors report extensive use of drugs to induce sedation, immobility, trance, and suggestibility, to induce dysphoric states (anxiety, nausea, pain) to punish resistance, to induce formation of self-states, and to bring victims to near-death, to block the formation of memories, and to create amnesia. Drugs that induce pleasure are used to reward compliance: "Sometimes they give you drugs that let you experience hell, sometimes they give you heroin" (Gresch, 2009).

Many survivors recall programming to make them perceive the presence of vials of mind-altering substances in their bodies that will be released into their bloodstream or brain if they violate programme injunctions. Particular self-states are often programmed to remain fixed in sedated or hallucinatory drugged states, and programmed to take executive control when victims begin to remember, or risk disclosing, their abuse. These form the basis of much anti-therapy programming.

The impact of electroshock

Electroshock may be the most common form of torture reported by mind control survivors. It appears to have two primary uses, to produce amnesia and to induce pain. MORI ID 146342 (1951) reveals:

> [a psychiatrist . . . a fully cleared Agency consultant] . . . stated that using this machine [Reiter] as an electroshock device with the convulsive treatment, he felt that he could guarantee amnesia for certain periods of time and . . . for any knowledge of use of the convulsive shock.

> [The doctor] stated that . . . lower current . . . produced in the individual excruciating pain and . . . the individual would be quite

willing to give information if threatened with the use of this machine.

Electroshock to the head sufficient to cause loss of consciousness and motor convulsions results in retrograde amnesia for the shock and preceding ten minutes (Shorter & Healy, 2007). None the less, there is evidence that the fear associated with the shock remains (Fox, 1993), as in fear conditioning. It follows that shock might cause programming to be registered fairly indelibly, albeit unconsciously.

Tien and Cameron used electroshock to respectively "erase" and "depattern" the mind. Post-electroshock, both found the mind more receptive to suggestion, consistent with survivor reports.

Many survivors report extensive use of electroshock to condition behaviour and to induce new self-states to form, often to their genitals and extremities. Gresch (2009, personal communication) states,

> I was tortured with electricity most of the time. Most survivors will probably report electric torture at the genitals . . . The perpetrator has a hand gear with which he can lead electricity to the penis or vagina of his victim.

Shock level is easily modulated. Threats to increase shock, promises to stop, etc., ensure compliance. It is easily classically conditioned to neutral stimuli that can be used as triggers. An electrician explains,

> The mental portion of shock is so intense . . . My cell phone vibrates and I get a fear reaction. It contracts the whole body. I can't think of any other form of torture that would give a torturer any more control.

Coercive hypnosis and manipulation of the imagination

Survivors report that hypnosis is the basis of much mind-control. MKULTRA documents provide extensive evidence of CIA interest in covert, coercive hypnosis (1) to block conscious processing and induce amnesia, (2) to induce dissociative states, (3) to make individuals execute "unethical actions", combined with drugs, after electroshock, during sleep, with auditory and visual stimuli, and after physical duress such as forced wakeful states, and (4) to create post-hypnotic assassins (MORI ID 144686, 017395, 017441, 190691, 190713). Estabrooks, one of the MKULTRA doctors, "publicly acknowledged the building of Manchurian Candidates" (Ross, 2000, p. 159).

Research has shown that one type of highly responsive hypnotic subject, the "amnesia-prone" individual, is likely to have been abused as a child and to have dissociative symptoms (Barber, 2000).

Mind control survivors are dissociation-prone, amnesia-prone, and fear-conditioned to submit to their trainers. Receptiveness to hypnosis "involves the intentional evocation of a special state characterized by focused attention" (Putnam & Carlson, 2002). Survivors are primed for states of intense, narrow attention to environmental cues to ensure survival. A psychologist-survivor (2008) explains, "Fear focuses attention intensely, and survival information is encoded deeply."

Rutz (2003) explains that her programming was eventually accomplished with hypnosis alone:

> All the programming that was done to me by the CIA and Illuminati was trauma-based using things like electroshock, sensory deprivation, and drugs. Later the trauma wasn't necessary, only hypnosis accomplished with implanted triggers and occasional tune-ups . . .

Rutz reports that Gottlieb, her programmer, also induced new self-states, "Baby" and "Guy", to form through hypnotic commands unaccompanied by torture.

Preschool children often make little distinction between reality and fantasy, actual events and pretend play. Programming begun in early childhood exploits their magical thinking and high hypnotizability. Programmers know that fantastic perceptions and beliefs "implanted" in the first four years of life will "stick", especially if "installed" in self-states dissociated from the host. Effects are enhanced by dependence on the programmer, "attaching" ominous entities, models, hallucinogens, and use of film.

This vignette illustrates the suggestibility of a frightened young child. Until she remembered this event, she was paralysed by the sight of maggots:

[T]here was beating and rape at the [abusers' house] that generally ended with the body having to clean up the rotten fruit [with maggots]. There was the same basic message . . . every time. They told her the maggots were the first sign they knew the body was talking. They [abusers] would send that to the body. It was the first warning . . . "The truth of speaking out carries on the wings of the flies". Then, the flies would bring back the warning . . . They said, "Flies are not of nature; they are witnesses to death, that's what creates the maggots, to eat the dead body."

Survivor Lynn Schirmer (2008, personal communication) explains use of story characters to develop self-states:

Elements of the Wizard of Oz movie were used in programming, especially the bit (in my case) about having no brain. Generally this was used to remind major alters inside of their limitations, that they can't access certain parts or memories, and calls up programming that induces a hazy air-headed feeling. They actually played the little Tin man song in the lab room.

Much programming relies on illusions and films, often combined with torture and drugs to increase suggestibility. Programmer goals in staging these events include making self-states perceive (1) that their abusers have magical power, usually over life and death; (2) that a harmful object or entity was installed; (3) that the victim was tortured, as in the film/drama; (4) that the victim behaved as in the film, for example, sexual films to build sexual alters, concentration camp films to form prisoner or torturer alters; (5) that others were killed due to victim disobedience; (6) that the victim harmed or killed others; (7) that personalities have died; (8) that the victim has powers of astral travel and psychic assassination.

Many survivors report being drugged, strapped to an electroshock device, and forced to watch a film that shows a child with similar features strapped to the same device. Victims believe they are watching themselves. One survivor described a camera pointing at her to further cement the illusion. Terror and helplessness are compounded because no movement or vocalization effects the "self" in the film.

Many survivors who initially believed they were tortured in Nazi concentration camps later realized that these memories were black and white and that a number flashed at the beginning of the memory. They then realized that they were forced to watch a Second World War Nazi film.

In her *Kabalah-Training Document*, this anonymous survivor describes her programmers' tricks:

> The perpetrators believe that when the eyelids are closed the light that is seen through them confuses the mind making it unable to tell the difference between reality and fantasy. You can tell them they have been abducted by aliens and tell them what they are seeing in the alien ship. You can tell them that they have had surgery, and that a device for keeping track of them is hidden under their scalp. You can tell them that the eye of Lucifer has been placed in their stomachs to keep an eye on them . . . As long as a small cut or scar of some kind is done at the same time, they will believe the eye of Lucifer has been placed in their stomachs to keep an eye on them, and they will believe it forever.

Survivor Patricia Baird Clark (2001) describes use of models and hypnosis to install her inner world:

> . . . a child may be . . . shown a castle . . . She spends several days in the castle going through painful, terrifying rituals in many of the rooms. She is forced to memorize the castle's entire layout. There will be a small replica of the castle much like an architectural model . . . Once this has been memorized, she is subjected to magic surgery. A tiny replica of the castle is shown to the child and she is told that it is being placed inside. The castle is now "within" . . . In this person's inner world she can now walk through the rooms and this castle has become as real to her in the spiritual dimension as it had been in the physical world.

> In subsequent rituals . . . the alters formed will be assigned to live in various rooms. These rooms are guarded by demons and booby traps are placed in strategic places so there is no escape . . . These castles have cold, dark dungeons filled with rats and snakes along with torture rooms . . .

Manipulation of attachment needs

Fear-driven attachment to one's abusers is endemic to severe abuse. Van der Kolk (1989) explains, ". . . children in particular, seek increased attachment in the face of external danger . . . When there is no access to ordinary sources of comfort, people may turn toward their tormentors" (p. 396).

In extreme abuse, appeasing the abuser subverts all self-advocacy. Schwartz (2000) explains, "The shocking absence of any anger at the perpetrators is entrenched and stays intact, as though prolonged immersion in sadistic abuse and extreme trauma bonding have almost completely reversed the self-protection system of the survivor" (p. 314).

Most mind control survivors recall their programmers developing bonds with key ego states beginning in the first few years of life as long-term tools of control, often designating themselves as "Daddy" or "Mummy" of particular ego states. Carol Rutz recalls Sidney Gottlieb telling her new alter, "Baby",

> "I am you mammer and your papper. You love only me, and I am the only one who loves you. I feed you and hold you, and you are mine alone" . . . Our baby part grew to love and depend on "Daddy Sid" as her only source of love and nourishment. From that day forward, a deep bonding took place . . . No matter what experiment he was to make me a part of, I would love and remain loyal to the man who my baby alter considered sole supplier of the basics of life, food, and love. [Rutz, 2001, p. 19]

A psychologist-survivor (2009) explains the readiness of newly formed states to bond to abusers:

> The newly formed tabula-rasa state will naturally attach to the abuser. This is a survival-based physiologically driven bonding response. If the abuser says; "You are Samantha, I am your Daddy, I love you, you belong to me, you will come when I call," this is taken in uncritically.

Consistent with object relations and attachment theory, Gresch believes that identity develops within significant relationships. For self-states induced to form within torture, the significant other is the programmer. Accordingly, it defines itself by the interactions within that moulding process, whether that be stories, hypnotism, torture-based conditioning, etc. By design, it has no motives of its own, except to avoid torture through complete submission to the abuser.

"Good cop–bad cop" and intermittent reinforcement are also used to build bonds. Children "excuse" and dissociate massive amounts of abuse to earn a pittance of highly "conditional" love. Svali explains,

> [T]he child is left alone, for . . . hours, to an entire day as the child grows older. If the child begs the adult to stay, and not leave, or screams, the child is beaten . . . The trainer will then "rescue" the child, feed and give it something to drink and bond with the child as their "saviour". [1996]

Svali (*ibid.*) explains that her abusers conditioned babies to associate nurturing and attention with night-time and rituals, and abandonment with daytime, a time of no rituals, so that the infant "eventually will associate cult gatherings with feelings of security".

Bonds of romantic love are also exploited, including ritual marriages between ego states and key abusers. Two children are sometimes married to exploit each child for long-term control of both. Such "weddings" often include exchange of bodily fluids to "attach" the spirits of each child to the other.

Programmers understand that genuine loving bonds are a great threat to ongoing control. The need for love may override the fear of torture, helping victims break free. So, sophisticated abusers seek to extinguish all hope for love. Protectors may be impersonated, or drugged and brought to events, to make them appear as abusers.

Set-ups are used to destroy trust in law enforcement and child protection. One victim was made to believe that fire sirens meant that her abusers were watching. Police sirens played during abuse, and abusers in police uniforms, further cement fear. Many abuser groups include actual police officers.

Psychotherapy may be the greatest threat to programming. Many survivors report that when they begin therapy, their abusers intensify their programming to reinforce "Don't remember–Don't tell" programming and to bolster "reporter" self-states to monitor any threats to programme integrity.

Exploitation of defensive identification with the aggressor

Mind control victims are essentially hostages, dependent on their abusers for their lives. Accordingly, ego states usually form who deny their own needs and identify with their abusers (Frankel & O'Hearn, 1996). Such ego-states may align with ideologies of their abusers (Stockholm Syndrome), including "national security" and spiritual ideologies, and often terrorize other self-states internally.

Programmers build on these defensive and survival responses, with characteristic pre-meditation, to serve their own ends.

Svali (1996) explains,

> Many trainers will put themselves in the person, over the internal programmers or trainers ... The survivor may be horrified to find a representative of one of their worst perpetrators inside, but this was a survival mechanism ... The survivor may mimic accents, mannerisms, even claim the perpetrator's life history as their own.

Ritual abuse and mind control victims are usually forced to harm others as soon as physically able. Toddlers are made to "kill" animals, even if their hands must be forced. "Claims" or names designating them as "Murderer", "Evil", etc., "cement" these beliefs in targeted self-states.

No-win double-binds force victims to believe they freely "chose" to abuse others. Survivor Lois Einhorn, PhD (2006), explains,

> I continually face "choices" as my parents ask me unanswerable questions: "Do you want to be hit or hit your sister?" "Do you want to have darts thrown at your front or throw them at your sister's front?" "Do you want to have a wire hanger put in you or do this to an animal?" ... Through being hit with a switch, we play, "How high can we make my little tushi jump?" My father, mother, and sister each take turns and keep score. If my sister loses, she is hit further. [p. 4]

Rage is manipulated to form abuser alters. Many survivors report being subjected to days-long torture to induce rage-filled parts to form, who are then trained as soldiers or warriors. Svali (1996) explains:

> ... The child is severely beaten, for a long period of time, by the trainer, then told to hit the other child in the room, or they will be beaten further. If the child refuses, it is punished severely, the other

child is punished as well, then the child is told to punish the other child. If the child continues to refuse, or cries, or tries to hit the trainer instead, they will continue to be beaten severely, and told to hit the other child, to direct its anger at the other child. This step is repeated until the child finally complies . . . The child will be taught that this is the acceptable outlet for the aggressive impulses and rage that are created by the brutality the child is constantly being exposed to.

Many abuser groups falsely promise key ego states that if they are loyal and obedient, they will eventually attain positions of power and reduced abuse. Most survivors have ego states who believe they were "chosen" for priest and priestess positions. These ego states are often amnestic for much of their early abuse, and only later realize that positions of power in their abuser group are only earned by "being able to take more pain" than other members.

Many abuser groups ultimately seek to develop individuals who consciously choose to be abusers. In the following description, Kernberg (1994) explains that the antisocial personality develops in a world of sadistic persecutors. This accurately depicts the world of mind control victims:

> The antisocial personality proper may be conceived as a characterologic structure so dominated by hatred that primitive, split-off idealizations are no longer possible, the world is populated exclusively by hated, hateful, sadistic persecutors, and to triumph in such a terrifying world can only occur by becoming oneself a hateful persecutor as the only alternative to destruction and suicide. [p. 701]

Svali (1996) explains that her abusers subjected children to "betrayal programming" to squelch all loving bonds and to create a world limited to "hated, hateful, sadistic persecutors" to yield an antisocial psychic structure, a "willing" persecutor. Young children were given "saviours", only to have these adults later betray them. Children were given so-called "twins" with whom to develop close bonds, only to be later forced to hurt or kill that "twin".

Schwartz (2000) explains that addiction to power is the outcome in such sub-cultures:

> Those who have not been personally exposed to those extremes may be unable fully to appreciate the compelling, corrupting,

degenerative spiral of extreme power obsessions. History has shown that once an individual or group becomes inflated with power (Hitler, Idi Amin, Pol Pot, the Duvaliers, Stalin, to name a few), a pattern of extravagant sadism, wanton cruelty, and irrational and ultimately self-destructive binges of exhibitionistic violence leads to eventual explosion or collapse. History has yet to reveal that these same diabolical dynamics are at work outside the context of war and politics—in perpetrator groups inflicting their power on children worldwide in the form of unimaginable abuse. [p. 319]

Manipulation of "free will" and "the spirit"

The concepts of "free will" and "the spirit" diverge from the more traditional psychological concepts discussed thus far. However, many mind-control survivors report that the will and spirit were the most sought-after prizes of their abusers.

Gresch (personal communication, 2009) explains that programmers go to great lengths to get victims to submit to their will:

The goal of mind control is total obedience. But, the absolute sovereign of the inner world is the individual. A human being can't be totally obedient unless he or she has decided to be. So the torturer must make his victim believe that total obedience is the best choice ... An artfully tailored system of mechanisms subconsciously links every idea to resist with the experience of annihilating torture.

Victims of espionage-based mind control describe most of their programmers as strict behaviourists and brain scientists who exclusively seek control of the mind and will.

Abusive cults also seek to control the spirit. This survivor recounts use of drugs, hypnosis, formal "claims" and "attachments" to "trap" her spirit: "He drugged me. He said that he put my heart [spirit] in a chest with a lock. He put his heart over my heart, and said, 'Your heart is mine, my heart is yours, I hold the key to your heart."

Survivors of both espionage and ritual groups commonly report "anti-God" programming. Faith in a loving God provides hope and support, both threats to mind control. Programmers mix torture and illusion to induce fear of God. Some victims report electroshock by the "hand of God". Many victims are programmed to invert all Judeo-Christian terms, to reverse "God" and "Satan", love and hate, and all prayers. Victims commonly experience aversions to God, religion, and houses of worship. In sophisticated witchcraft abuse, a full half of the self-state system may reject God as a threat.

Both technological and spiritual programmers manipulate victims into defining themselves as shameful, evil, and unworthy of belonging anywhere but in the abuser group. Fotheringham (2008) explains that her abusers' Catch-22 set-ups left her with "soul-deadening shame":

> At age 5, the death and dissection of a kitten was proof of the black soldier alter being able to "stomach the job," and at 6, a test proving "family loyalty" forced a choice for the dark blue alter between letting my little brother get hurt or letting our pet rabbit suffer and die . . . [A]ny capitulation in such double-bind situations left me with crippling, soul-deadening shame, guilt, powerlessness and helplessness, especially in the presence of people with authority or "good, decent people." [p. 507]

This psychologist-survivor (2009) describes the Machiavellian tactics used to make her feel aligned with the devil:

> They put me in a wooden casket and buried me . . . I heard the sound of shovels full of dirt hitting the top of the casket in a rhythm. Then I heard nothing. It was pitch-black dark. It was hard to breathe because there was dust in the air. Then, it goes blank. I believe I passed out from terror, lack of air, and believing I was dead . . . Then, I heard a sound and it was faint, then louder, then finally a shovel hitting the casket . . . I was yanked out by the same person who buried me. He said that people do not come back from the dead unless they make a deal with the devil, and he laughed in a sneering way. Then he said I had a choice. He said, "Get back in the casket, or do X." This happened many times. The things I had to do to stay out of the casket were horrible, including sexual acts using animal parts, and hurting other people and animals. If I would not do as he said or get in the casket willingly, he would force me into the casket with spiders. When I came out, he said that I was not bitten because spiders do not bite people with bad blood. If I did the abuse he ordered, he said, "Look what you did, you are

just like us, you are as evil as us, if you ever tell anyone, they will know you are as evil as us."

The "soul-deadening shame" of recalling the harm done to others is the point where many survivors abandon their healing journeys, a trap intentionally set by programmers. Schwartz (2000) explains that in victims who were made to harm others, "Identifying with abusers' ideologies and motivations not only sustains attachment [to abusers], but allows victims to endure excruciating, otherwise intolerable guilt and shame" (p. 299). Defensive dissociation of the excruciating pain of facing that one harmed another human being may be the greatest driving force behind the compulsion to repeat evil in general.

Psychotherapeutic approaches to overcoming mind control

In my experience, the process of discovering and overcoming programming is facilitated by having as much knowledge of programming as possible, means of working with survivors to obtain information about their programming, methods to effect deep inner change such that the programming is no longer effective, and stabilization and containment strategies to support the survivor during these processes.

I believe that most people need the support of another person to become conscious of, and to overcome, programming. This is normally a therapist, but is sometimes a clergyperson, friend, or significant other. For some survivor-therapists, it is a colleague. But rarely can a survivor look at programming trauma alone, even with established psychotherapeutic tools and a strong spiritual base. It is usually too painful, frightening, and disorientating to face without an external anchor for support.

"Don't remember", "Don't tell", and anti-therapy programming

Based on my work with clients and my interviews with other survivors, I have come to believe that programmers put as much, or greater, effort into "cover-up" programming to try to keep their

victims from developing conscious awareness of their programming as they put into the agenda-driven programming itself. When
"Don't remember" and "Don't tell" programming are overcome,
the rest of the programming is much more easily made conscious
and overcome.

Thus, when "Don't remember" and "Don't tell" programming
are "activated", this not a time-wasting obstacle, but a primary
problem requiring resolution. Working through this programming
can be understood as an opportunity to analyse the resistance.
Thompson (2004) explains, "[A]nalysts who 'analyze' the resistance
endeavor to turn the tables on it by making the resistance, not
merely an artifact of the treatment, but the focus of it" (p. 130).

When working with survivors of mind control, what we
normally think of as "resistance" is compounded by the fact that it
was deliberately "installed" and is "fuelled" by dissociated self-
states who perceive their abuse as ongoing. By abuser design, the
determinants of this resistance are less consciously available. But,
the source of this resistance is the very programming we seek to
resolve.

It is important not to "blame the survivor" for these "blocks".
High motivation is necessary to resolve programming, but is
usually not enough alone.

Many well-meaning clergy make the mistake of believing that
free will, deep spiritual faith, and asking God to reveal the truth
should be enough to discover and resolve all programming. But
programmers understand the power of faith and programme their
victims against God. Even deeply religious survivors often struggle
with aversive reactions to the word "God", prayer, etc., based in
unconscious anti-God programming. For some survivors, choosing
an atypical word to refer to God reduces the effects of such programming. For others, more creative circumventions are required.

In ritual abuse groups low in programming sophistication,
"don't remember" programming may be the most severe, deeply
buried trauma. A victim of such a group was attempting to work
through a ritual when she saw flashes of coloured light. In exploring the meaning of the lights, she recalled, "You tell, you die." She
discovered that as a small child, she had begun to tell an aunt of her
abuse. Her abusers took her to more advanced programmers to
silence her. These programmers electroshocked her repeatedly, each

time saying, "You tell, you die." Once this became conscious, she was able to change these words to "I choose to live". With support and guidance for each step, she was able to ask her spiritual source to go into the programming room, push the abusers away from herself, destroy the electroshock equipment, pick up the self-states formed by this trauma, and bring them to an inner healing place she had already created. Thereafter, the only "blocks" while working through the rituals were perceived "spiritual attachments" from rituals.

Gresch (personal communication, 2009), explains that one of his self-states was programmed to prevent any progress in psychotherapy:

> One of my "alters" was trained to behave properly in psychotherapeutic situations. I was conditioned to refrain from psychotherapy, but the perpetrators know that no programming is perfect. So they teach their slaves how to be a very, very compliant, and sometimes a resistant client who gives his or her therapist the feeling of healing and progress where there really is none. Be sure that whenever in a psychotherapeutic situation, alters appear and execute their programs. If the survivor is not recalling and defying the abuse and programming, then the perpetrators are holding the reins.

Many survivors are also programmed against the use of hypnosis by anyone but their programmers and handlers, since hypnosis is an effective means of obtaining information from the unconscious mind and in overcoming programming. Hypnosis is also a basic tool in programming and, therefore, very frightening to many survivors. Many therapists have learned to never use formal hypnosis or the term, "hypnosis", when working with mind control survivors. However, this does not limit the therapy process in that survivors of mind control are generally adept at narrowing and intensifying the focus of their attention, as in hypnosis, and readily use imagery of their own volition.

Knowledge of programming

I believe that therapists working with survivors of mind control must be students of programming. The more we understand, the more we recognize signs of various kinds of programming, and the more easily we can formulate the right questions to help our clients discover their programming. When we demonstrate some level of comfort in asking about programming and working with it, we begin to earn the trust of dissociated self-states.

I believe that complete "neutrality" and use of only open-ended questions has a high risk of promoting many "false negatives" in ritually abused and programmed clients. I have observed that neutral questions, such as, "and then what happened?", often leave clients too alone in their fear, causing much trauma to remain dissociated, often indefinitely. Focused questions allow for more material to come forward. For example, asking, "Was anyone else involved?", lets survivors know we are open to hearing of multi-perpetrator abuse. Asking, "Was it perceived that anything was attached in that abuse?", lets survivors know we are open to work with perceived spiritual aspects of the abuse. Asking whether anything was done to intentionally control the mind opens the subject of mind control.

Proponents of "false memory syndrome" will argue that we should not formulate questions based on prior knowledge, that this influences our clients to produce false memories. I agree there is a risk of generating confusion and acquiescence if therapists ask questions that assume the unstated. However, questions that are too general often fail to communicate that the therapist understands enough to help.

For example, if a client recalls torture in a concentration camp, questions about whether the memory is in colour or black and white may reveal that the memory involved viewing an old film. One survivor recalled that Satan revived a dead animal. When asked about the position of the body and what the body was wearing, she recalled being strapped in a chair rigged for torture and wearing a helmet with virtual reality goggles.

A more complex example is sophisticated electroshock programming. One or more coloured wires might be attached to the chest, head, genitals, extremities, etc. Programmed self-states may perceive that they are wired together and that they can only be detached from the electroshock device by cutting the wires in a particular order, turning down the electricity in specified increments, removing attached explosive devices, etc. If done out of order, programmed self-states might perceive the explosive devices at the end of the wires to detonate. Informed questions can help a client feel safe enough to remember this kind of programming: for example, "Where are the wires connected to [each alter]?", "How many wires are connected to [each location]?", "What are the colours of those wires?", "Is there anything at the end of that wire?", "Do any wires connect one [alter] to another?", "Is there anything more we need to know about the wires?" In contrast, the reliability of the information might be weakened and fear may be induced by asking, "Is there an explosive device at the end of that wire?"

Informed questions are also helpful in working through abusive rituals. Significant information may be learned by asking who dressed the child and how. Witchcraft abusers often place jewellery, painted words, body substances, etc., on victims to "attach" themselves. It may help to ask who brought the child to the event, who was there, if artefacts were used and their significance, etc. Since abusers often compete for spiritual dominance of victims, it is often revealing to ask, "Did anyone else do anything to harm the child before or after this event?" If such questions are not asked, survivors will sometimes work through a ritual without discovering and resolving the most adverse and controlling elements.

The more we know about programming, the more skilfully we can also side-step programmed self-destruction, health, and mental health consequences. The host may be determined to defy all such programming. However, the entire programmed purpose of some self-states is to trigger punishment programming, and these functions are executed independently of the host.

For example, complex programmes have "failsafes", such as bombs, booby-traps, back-ups, and re-sets. Programmes may be networked to activate multiple programmes if there is interference with any one programme. Sophisticated programmers install removal procedures, including codes, so they can remove, replace, and redo programmes. Removal of such programmes requires a cautious, methodical approach. If the programmer said a specific removal code must be used, the affected self-states often perceive that only that exact code can erase that programme. To these self-states, the programmer may be perceived as God. Generally, to remove such programming, the exact code must be found, the programmed removal steps followed, and each element undone within the reality of the programmed self-states.

I will not minimize the difficulty of researching programming. "Don't remember" programming makes reliable information hard to come by. And there are so many kinds of programmes, it is a daunting task. Additionally, there is much misinformation, as well as probably deliberate disinformation, on the Internet.

None the less, we can learn much from survivors' written accounts and from consultation with survivors and colleagues. Information about specific forms of programming is often too sensitive for large Internet forums. There is a risk that specific case examples can get back to a client's abusers and that those abusers may retaliate against that client for "telling". Inexperienced therapists may disclose too much detail to clients, resulting in fear, confusion, or negative programming consequences. Generally, therapists working with mind control survivors "play our cards close to our chests" so that we do not help programmers outpace us with their strategies. As one survivor told me, "You are part of the experiment."

Establishing safety

It has been my experience that almost all survivors of ritual abuse and mind control benefit from the use of a formal process to "protect the space" prior to depth therapy work to overcome programming.

I tell my clients that when they are in my office, it is a place dedicated solely to their healing, and that both they and I have the right and the power to assert our will to protect the sanctity of this place from anyone or anything that might intend otherwise.

Most clients benefit from the use of a formal declaration or prayer for this purpose. For many non-religious clients, their declaration is simply a setting of an intention. It may begin with, "By my will", "I declare", etc. Religious clients may do the same, or pray to, or in the name of, their spiritual source.

Before depth work, I ask my clients if they want to say their declaration/prayer or have me say it. Almost always, they choose for me to say it. The effect is very calming and focusing.

This sample declaration is by an atheist:

> All energies and entities that are not part of our true self must leave
> immediately to at least 50 feet away from all sides of this place. This
> is my place to heal. No entry of any kind is permitted for any
> reason. Nothing can be seen, heard, or felt in any way by any entity
> not a part of our self. I do not permit any thoughts, distortions,
> manipulations, videos, pictures, fears, sickness, pain, or other feel-
> ings to enter. This is my place of healing. All entities must comply.

Using this declaration, material could be discovered and processed
that was previously blocked. When, none the less, the work became
blocked, reasserting the declaration unblocked it.

This prayer/declaration is by a survivor with a broad-based, *vs.*
specifically religious, faith in God:

> In God's Divine Light and Love, I command any parts not truly my
> creation that do not serve the truth and light of the Creator to leave
> now, never to return. I bless them and send them back to their
> source and their family.

Clients who discover victimization by witchcraft cults often
declare or pray protection against the kinds of spiritual attack used
by such abusers, including refusing parts of their abusers' spirits,
their demons, curses, hexes, vexes, threats, closing portals, and
turning back astral pathways. Victims of such cults often sense that
particular "forms of evil" are being sent as we begin a session, and
occasionally within the work. This is usually more easily managed
than a "block" based in prior spiritual programming, which usually
must be made conscious and resolved. Most clients find that they
need only, in prayer or declaration, refuse to allow each form of perceived attack. This generally "clears" the way for the work to
proceed and reduces any perceived interference later in the session.

Making programming conscious

Programming works when it remains intact and undisturbed in
dissociated self-states and in the unconscious mind. Conversely,
programming is disabled when it becomes conscious and is then
defied or changed.

I use the term "defiance" to refer to the assertion of one's will against doing or believing as one's abusers and programmers directed, trained, conditioned, hypno-suggested, claimed, etc. I use "change" to refer to making modifications in the unconscious mind, inner world, or self-states. The survivor may relocate a self-state from a site of torture to a healing place in the inner world. Programmed directives and claims can be changed to self-affirming statements, as in the survivor who replaced, "You tell, you die", with "I choose to live". Toxins, explosive substances, and drugs can be removed in prayer by a spiritual source or "beamed out" as per *Star Trek*. Programme removal codes can "erase" programmed structures from the internal landscape. Programme reset codes can be changed to impossible stimuli, for example, a one-inch tall baby giraffe with peppermint breath whistling Dixie. Perceived malevolent human spirits and entities can be expelled by assertion of will or prayer. Once these modifications are made in the inner world, they tend to "stick" and do not require ongoing conscious effort. What programmers initially established in the inner world through torture, illusion, and hypno-suggestion, the survivor now re-sculpts in ways that serve the self.

Another necessary quality is the desire, perhaps the decision, to face the past trauma. The significance of this decision is eloquently shared here by Rutz (2003). I share this with many clients:

> In those early days as the bits and pieces of my life were expressed on the pages of my journal I was afraid all of the time—24–7. I was flooded with memories, flashbacks, and nightmares. Fear was my number one major obstacle to overcome before any real work could be done. I was afraid of remembering and I was afraid not to remember. I was afraid the cult would somehow know I was talking and send someone to exterminate me. I was afraid the memories were really true. I was afraid I was a liar and for some reason making it all up. I eventually came to accept and know that no matter what; I had already lived through the worst. Remembering, understanding, feeling and incorporating those experiences was the pathway I walked to slowly integrate my alters.

> Fear consumed me until I finally let go and allowed the details of my life to flow from my mind to the paper and then in therapy through my mouth. I found that letting my alters finally have a voice and speak the truth was the only way through the fear. My

alters found painting and drawing to be a perfect expression for getting scenes recorded—peoples [*sic*] faces, places, buildings, ceremonies. I never knew what was going to be painted or drawn, I just gave my alters free reign. Years later when I actually was able to match real people and places with these, the validation was overwhelmingly powerful and helped me to understand what truly happened to me.

"Who" works in therapy to overcome programming?

The work of becoming conscious of programming, defying and changing it, is accomplished in a highly focused mental state. The intense affect associated with discovering this trauma must be either tolerated, distanced from defensively, symbolically contained, or regulated with intense cognitive focus, as LeDoux (1996) suggests, "getting the cortex to control the amygdala". At the close of the session, the survivor is usually both physically and mentally exhausted.

"Who" in the self-state system needs to do this work? Who can tolerate it?

For many years, I thought that the host must be the ego state to work with in therapy to discover and resolve programming. This was based on work with a number of survivors with strong hosts who embodied much "true self" and who functioned somewhat as a hub for the entire self-state system.

However, in some cases, the host functions more as a superficial shell, like a chameleon adapting to each setting, or as a programmed façade, than as "true self" acting on its own behalf. This kind of host is inadequately connected to the survivor's needs and history, and lacks the emotional forbearance to face the abuse. However, as other ego-states successfully address programming, an initially weak host often becomes more "real", "full", and able to tolerate painful and frightening memories.

Relatively developed ego states with a significant sense of self that extends beyond the torture they endured, and who seek the highest good for the whole self, can sometimes engage in therapy to work through programming. In some cases, these are "hard", "tough", rebellious ego states, not aligned with the aggressor, but true advocates for the self. Their detachment from vulnerable emotions is a tool that often helps them confront memories of torture.

Sometimes, ego states originally heavily programmed for system oversight functions decide to defy their abusers and change "sides". These ego states know much more than their own experience, having been programmed for key monitoring functions, such as recorder and reporter alters, or regulatory functions, such as alters that control "switching" between the host and programmed self-states, or system leadership roles, such as alters with significant status in their abuser groups.

Gresch (personal communication, 2009) worked through his programming with the help of his "mediator", programmed as system administrator to (1) steer his front personality, which was only a staged façade, and keep it amnestic for the programming, (2) deactivate his "kernel" (original self), and (3) ensure that his torture-hypno-conditioned alters, all off-shoots of the mediator, executed their duties as directed. When the mediator decided to defy his programmers, its knowledge of the system helped overcome the programming.

Miller (2008) discusses the importance of working with system leaders, especially those who believed their abusers' lies, false promises, and threats, to discover their abusers' deceptions and to gain the co-operation of the alters beneath them in the internal hierarchy. Then, internal observer and recorder alters can assist the therapist in selecting the most critical memories that need to be worked through.

Fotheringham (2008) had a self-created record keeper who hid boxes of records unbeknown to her abusers. This alter was able to later help her work through memories of the abuse:

> Unbeknownst to my handler and trainers, a record keeper alter split off and got stuck at age eight, due to an overload of righteous outrage and hate from witnessing and recording too much hateful, horrific wrongness and injustice. Most of the "boxes of records" were kept by this alter and hidden in my inner tunnels. Luckily, "files in folders" had recently been introduced and instituted as the main storage system of my inner world, so this absence amazingly went unnoted, and the records remained pure and intact until this alter was discovered in my late 30's [sic]. As a result of this

particular split, a significant piece of my natural activist/defender voice escaped later "adjustments and fine-tuning," and was never caught in the "shutdown and discard" programming which happened later. [p. 510]

Many survivors have the experience that parts of the self went out-of-body during abusive events and saw the events from a bird's eye-view. Other ego states were perceived to hide within the body as they watched the abuse. From these vantage points, these parts often "see" through abusers' illusions, disguises, tricks, film, etc., and have more knowledge than directly tortured self-states.

Victims of abusive witchcraft often have a hidden ego state who was largely self-created to fend for itself in the world of abusers. This ego state often "watches" the abuse as it occurs. At some point, especially within a respectful therapy relationship, this part may question the world-view, theology, and agenda of the abusers. This part can be of tremendous help in resolving programming if it joins forces with the true self or a strong host. However, these significant kinds of shifts do not tend to happen early in the recovery process.

In many cases, memories of programming are initially registered in a multitude of self-states, and these alters join forces to process these. Many therapists invite all self-states affected by a particular event to meet in an internal therapy room to go through the event. Fotheringham (2008) explains,

> [E]xperiences were . . . often fragmented as they occurred. This meant that one alter could be "out" for an event, while one or more of [the] base alters "siphoned off" the feelings, emotional states, and/or pain that went with whatever was experienced, without truly being out in the body. Due to this, each alter's piece of the memory had to be accessed and addressed before the whole experience could be considered reclaimed and healed. [p. 497]

Fotheringham (personal communication, 2010) explains that her host and alters worked together to discover her programming. Her host provided intention and focus by deepening into whatever emotional or somatic state she was experiencing. She focused on the feeling and how she felt it in her body, asking, "What's this feeling about; where does it come from? What is it connected to? What is its root cause? What does this feeling have to tell me?" (see Watkins's "affect bridge", 1971, and "somatic bridge", 1992). Then, her trauma-bearing states, and states perceived to have observed the abuse, often from out of the body, would share the memories. She found that her emotions were, in essence, a synthesis of her trauma experiences, and her greatest tool in guiding her to discover her memories.

Rutz (personal communication, 2009) similarly found that all involved alters had to contribute to resolve their programming, often by initially addressing the fear of the alter in the greatest pain:

> [I]f it was a ritual abuse situation, it was possible that four or five alters would be part of it. One for the pain, one for the ritual, one for being transported, etc. etc. . . . I think that the reason many DID people have trouble recalling what happened to them is that you most always have many different alters as part of one situation. It is not possible to recall the entire event unless you get the perspective of each alter involved. If you can work through the fear of the alter presenting with all the pain, you have the possibility of actually reaching the rest. Many times I would remember events backwards, and then lastly put it all together and understand and feel the ramifications of it all.

In some cases, the above methods are adequate to discover and resolve programming. In other cases, many programmed self-states are "frozen" in time and space in sites of torture and are inaccessible to the survivor and therapist. If they "come forward", they often bring overwhelming pain, terror, and drugged states with them, restricting the capacity for mental focus, and flooding the psyche with their distress. Many self-states cannot participate because they are too fragmentary, limited to the function they originally served during the abuse to suffer pain or terror or perform a circumscribed behaviour.

Much programming is held in place by self-states in hiding. Many hide in terror. Some are hidden in compliance with torture-hypnotic directives to "go to" particular locales in the unconscious mind, and are now "too far away" to be reached, often behind walls or chasms installed in programming. Some survivors have groups of self-states programmed to internally "reside" apart from each other by programmers with different agendas. These groups are usually largely unknown to each other. Even "watchful" parts may not have been able to witness the entirety of some events.

In victims of ritual abuse, affected self-states often perceive themselves to be controlled by malevolent spiritual attachments. It is only after much of the "spiritual programming" is "undone" that these self-states feel "free" enough of spiritual evil to participate in therapy in any way.

So, in many cases, the survivor needs more than a strong host or other strong ego states to work through programming. "Don't talk", "Don't tell", and anti-therapy programming are aimed at silencing hosts and other key ego states. Registration of programming events is often spread across many self-states, many hidden. Some self-states are obedient or loyal to their abusers. Some believe the theology or illusions, tricks, and lies of their abusers. And some programming is placed directly in the unconscious mind, "beneath" the level of all self-states.

How can the survivor overcome these barriers to consciously processing their programming?

Obtaining a meta-view

One solution to many of these obstacles is to work with the survivor to develop a means of obtaining a meta-view of the survivor's trauma history and self-state system. A few methods to achieve a meta-view include work with internal self helpers (ISHes), work with a strong self-reflective "true self", work with the unconscious mind, and work with the survivor's spiritual source. These are somewhat overlapping constructs and each survivor and therapist will define them differently.

An internal self helper may be considered a specialized ego state or a superconsciousness beyond ego states. Many therapists and clients understand it as spiritual in nature; others understand it in purely psychological terms. Conceptions of the ISH include the spiritual self, spirit, soul, the part connected to God, a higher self, source of inner wisdom, inner guide, co-therapist, observing ego, hidden observer, central organizing force, an ego-state aware of all other self-states (a hub), holder of all memory and life experience, and the unconscious or subconscious mind itself (Adams, 1989; Comstock, 1991).

Some survivors and therapists ask why the wise, system-savvy ISH cannot be the host. My observation is that ISHs expend great mental energy to be "up front". They can sustain this only briefly, although this can be extended, especially within the support of a therapy relationship.

In some people, the "true self" and ISH are much the same. For others, an ISH is a specialized ego state that one accesses in a highly focused or meditative state, while the "true self" is broader in scope. In internal family systems therapy, the "Self" is considered to be the undamaged core identity and the "system leader" a therapist to the "internal family" (Goulding & Schwartz, 1995; Nichols & Schwartz, 1991). Internal family systems therapists help clients move into the position of the "Self" to work with their dissociated ego states. For other therapists, the "true self" is viewed as something that must develop more gradually, through increased capacity for self-reflection, genuine expression of affect, integration of trauma memory, and increased critical thinking (Schwartz, 2000).

For Gresch, only his true self, whom he views as the "one-and-only person", could discover and overcome his programming. Gresch views all alters, including the host, as originating in this true self, and having long ago submitted to executing scripted roles in response to torture and training designed to break the will. When the survivor becomes aware that he or she "created alters" to comply with the abusers, this critical "break-through" allows the true self to make the choice to defy the programmers and discard the roles and alters. The most challenging step to this critical act of defiance is to reduce the fear that had kept these memories and the true self hidden (personal communication, 2009).

A third means of obtaining a meta-view is to work with the unconscious or subconscious mind (UM). Fortunately, it is not necessary for my purposes here to attempt to define the elusive UM. It will suffice to say that therapists and survivors who use the UM as a resource to work through trauma generally view it as a holder of all memory and information about all self-states. Many also view it as a source of wisdom, the spiritual self, and the connection to God.

Work with the client's spiritual source is also a means to obtain a meta-view. The spiritual source may be God of an established religion, a broader "higher power" or source of love, the spirit within, or light, love, truth, etc. Some survivors prefer an animal that symbolizes strength or protection. For some survivors, there are limits to the material that can be obtained through work with a spiritual source. For other survivors, one's spiritual source provides an effective meta-view.

Some survivors are able to focus inward to obtain a meta-view to make their programming conscious, and to overcome it, without the assistance of a therapist, friend, or loved one. They have usually already done a great deal of inner work on themselves, and they are usually currently safe. Some have a strong spiritual foundation. Some use art, writing, or sand trays to increase inner focus. Some need only the support of an empathic witness to do the work. Some describe having internal ISHs who are always working to undo programming.

These survivors are the exceptions. In my experience, most survivors cannot do meta-view work unassisted. It requires a state of deep internal focus and external support is needed to stay grounded. Most survivors also need help to structure and tolerate this hard work. I have found it tremendously helpful for the therapist to help the survivor develop a formal procedure to obtain a meta-view to discover programming, to provide much guidance in overcoming it, and to help contain noxious trauma-derived affect and somatic sensations that arise in the process.

Development of a formal procedure
to make programming conscious

Before beginning the hard work of making programming conscious and overcoming it, I spend a good deal of time working with clients to develop tools that create enough structure and safety to do this difficult work, that allow for a meta-view of trauma memory and the self-state system, and that facilitate resolution of programming. These tools include:

1. Obtaining a family tree and history, education and work history, areas of residence, etc., for future reference.
2. Creation of a formal declaration or prayer to "protect the space" at the start of depth work.
3. Maintaining deep respect for the client's free will. I often ask, "Is it your free will to do this work?" before processing

programming. During the work, I often ask, "Do I have permission to ask . . .?" The choice to proceed, in itself, helps to reduce anxiety and increase focus. It is important to avoid power struggles, even when there is risk of harm to self, even when re-contact with abusers may be imminent. Pressure to control any thoughts, feelings, or behaviour is likely to be experienced as reminiscent of abuser control. Efforts to control high-risk behaviours may be perceived as a promise of more protection than the therapist can provide, ultimately leading to disappointment, and can make the client feel disempowered or overly dependent on the therapist. The therapist can work with the survivor to increase safety, but the motivation to work to stay safe must originate in the survivor.

4.   Exploring the client's deepest values and spiritual beliefs to determine the role of this "spiritual source" in the work. Beliefs as non-specific as the right to freedom, truth, healing, or love for animals can be powerfully applied to resolve programming. Spiritual beliefs can help in protecting the safe place, containment strategies, effecting change in the inner world, "rescuing" states from sites of trauma, and for healing of traumatized states.

5.   Creating a container to store pain, fear, spinning, body fluids, and drugged and toxic states, in order to reduce flashbacks and flooding, and to side-step programming to re-experience trauma. I often say, "There is no value in reliving pain and fear; go ahead and place those in your container." For extreme torture, repeated guidance may be required, for example, "Continue to store the shock", or, "Reduce the spinning by half, reduce it by half again. Let me know if it has been stored." In some cases, noxious states and substances may need to be stored in separate containers. The client's spiritual source can also be used to contain or remove unwanted feelings and substances.

Rutz (2003) explains how she used a toy box to contain memories between sessions and how she learned to be able to "stay in the present" in therapy:

[We] all know how awful abreaction is, even though it is effective at allowing the alters to tell and getting a really accurate picture of what took place . . . [I]n the beginning I was doing nothing but abreacting. I would find myself in my mind in a room looking at a closed door. After opening the door for the first time I always knew I would find a traumatic scene from my past, generally where a new alter had been created.

When I left the therapists [sic] office I would have to put what I had been working on away, so that I could effectively live during the week without being bombarded by the new material. I created an internal safe place to put the memories that we worked on in each session so that I would not be flooded in between. It was a toy box and I would set a stuffed animal on top before I left the office. During the week we would journal or not, which ever felt safe, and then let the memories back out of the toy box again in therapy the following week. This was different from the safe place my alters eventually built to go to for healing.

Later after my therapist had attended a seminar we began using grounding techniques so that while I was remembering I could also remain in the present. This was much less painful and traumatic to the system and every bit as effective as pure abreaction. My grounding technique was really simple. I taught myself that when I would begin to abreact and lose total control, I would grab the arm of the chair and bring myself back to the awareness of where I was. That insured that I was still in the present, and this happened in the past and did not have the power to hurt me anymore.

6. Creating an inner place of healing or recovery, a place where self-states can be "rescued to" from the sites of their abuse, to physically and emotionally heal. This place can include nurturing ego states, spiritual help, pets, soothing things, etc. A pre-established healing place increases the capacity to discover programming, including lowering resistance posed by frightened self-states.

    Rutz (2003) explains how she used a healing place for alters to rest and heal and for grounding:

The same visualization that was used by perps for programming enabled us to undo that programming. We created a healing place inside where anyone who chose to could go and rest and get help from other alters in healing. I found parts that couldn't speak because of programming or being preverbal and a helper alter would agree to be used for the memory retrieval work. That part would remain grounded so that the emotional impact was not so overwhelming. I believe this is really important and could cause system wide shut down if we attempt to handle too much at one time.

7. Creating a place to do the work of making programming conscious and resolving it. A place devoted to this work greatly facilitates meta-view work. Some survivors readily create such a place. Others believe that there can never be any safe place. Some have been programmed against any inner safe place (Svali, 1996, Chapter Two). If a survivor feels such a place is not possible, I explain that many others initially felt the same way, yet created one. It is essential to maintain a stance of "We will create a way around every abuser intimidation and machination", in order to overcome programming.

The survivor decides "who" will work in this place. It may be one or more of a host, ISH, the "true self", etc. Prior to "going to" the working place, it often helps to have all other states go somewhere to be distracted, such as a playground.

Safety measures can be established to travel to this place, such as a secret entry or being taken by one's spiritual source. I suggest that the journey be made possible only when it is of their genuine free will and exclusively for the purpose of their healing, to prevent abuser coercion or threats being used to force survivors to reveal their place.

Additional security measures are needed with very fearful survivors. Once the designated ego states are in this place, I let them know that they can develop additional safeguards to further hide it from outside detection. Programmers install illusions, such as buildings, guards, locks, and internal barriers in victims' inner worlds to control them. Survivors can use this same imaginative capacity and malleability of their internal worlds to their own advantage. The survivor ultimately has more control of his/her inner world than a programmer ever could.

Fotheringham (2008, personal communication) explains how she created places for her healing:

As part of my healing, I adopted the use of structures for my own benefit. When I had a need for a specific alter or group of alters that could not be met within the already existing structures, or by adapting them for my purpose, one of my alters . . . would design a new structure to serve the needed purpose. I ended up with, among others, a Healing House with a Healing Hot Springs Hot Tub . . . a huge 4 story Discovery Lodge with an Intensive Care Unit and "Memory Processing Unit" (to ease extreme suffering of individual alters trapped in torture, by extracting and storing memories for later retrieval and processing), a Nursery (with soundproofed room for the one who screamed all the time) . . . and big, individually equipped dorm rooms for the various groups of children, and the 24 Rear Guardsmen who mostly became child-care-givers!

I suggest clients use their creative capacity to hide their working place from everyone, including me. Only the voice of the therapist need be heard there. I say, "Only you need to know how you hide this place. You can create a decoy, like a painting can hide a safe, like a secret-door bookcase can hide a room. Your first place can be a counterfeit with an illusion that makes it look like the work is stuck, with your true place anywhere in the universe, perhaps accessible only through your spiritual source."

Once the designated ego states are in the working place, it is important to help them feel "grounded" there so they do not relive the trauma memories being processed. I might say, "Feel where you are sitting, tell me what you see, what is the temperature, etc." While working, if the client begins to relive a memory, I remind them, "Stay in your working place without 'going into' the trauma."

A procedure should also be developed to help clients leave the working place at the close of the work, such as "locking" or otherwise securing it and grounding themselves back in the office.

Once back in the therapy room, most clients need to process the trauma they have discovered in more conscious, less intently focused, more emotional ways. Some clients choose to "leave" their memories in their working place until the next session. Over time, they develop increased tolerance for conscious memory of the trauma they are processing, and reserve this option for the most difficult material.

8.   Establishing procedures to obtain information while in the working place. Clients who work with an ISH or the "true self"

usually use a fairly straightforward process of choosing to work and deep focus on exploring the origins of particular symptoms or snippets of memory. Clients working with a spiritual source usually pray to be shown the truth about what happened. Clients working with the unconscious mind may simply get a sense of "knowing", or they may create additional imagery to know or see "answers" and images. One survivor lowered her questions in a bucket into a well that represented her unconscious mind; the bucket brought the answers or images forward. Others watch words or images on a television screen, read the answers from a book, etc.

Material to explore and kinds of questions to ask

Some survivors proceed to discover programming with a simple intention to know about anything that was done to control the self. It is often expeditious to focus on the most pivotal information as soon as possible, by asking something like: "What is the most important event to look at?", or to begin with the earliest programming, since it is often foundational for later programming.

More often, current material supplies the direction for the work: a disturbing thought or impulse, a flashbulb memory, a stimulus that "triggered" distress, a somatic sensation or symptom, a sense of fear or threat, a dream, symbols in art, writing, or sand trays, or efforts to understand a particular self-state.

In the early stages of using this process, and later as particularly sensitive information is broached, it is helpful to repeatedly ask, "Do I have permission to . . .", or, "Would it cause any harm to look at . . ."

Early in the process of doing this work, and at the beginning of a day's work, small, specific questions help to "grease the works" and are more manageable because the survivor is in a trance-like state, "somewhere" between the external and internal worlds, between mental clarity and dream-like primary process thought. Small, focused questions also reduce fear of remembering and telling.

Formulating questions is the real art of this work. Questions should be focused, yet not leading. Because this work requires such intense mental effort, it helps to repeat what the client just said within the next question: "And when [what client just said], what happened next?" (www.davidgrove.com/).

When beginning with current material, a good first question is whether that issue has something to do with a particular event. If the answer is yes, the next question might be, "Do I have permission to ask for the age of the body at the time of this event?" It helps to set the stage for the event by asking who dressed the child, who took the child there, whether it occurred outdoors or indoors, who was present, the position of the body, etc. These concrete details generally make the memory more accessible, and the survivor may then be able proceed in the order of what occurred.

Important areas to explore include how the child was abused and whether anything was done to put the child in an altered state of consciousness, for example, drugs, spinning, suffocation, near-death, etc. It is important to learn about what may have been placed on, or in, the body of the child. It is critical to determine whether new self-states were formed, whether their purpose was to serve the self or the abusers, and the degree the abusers used these newly formed self-states for their purposes. A useful question is, "For what purpose, or in response to what, was this part created?" It is important to discover the words spoken to harm, control, define, or name self-states. Sometimes, it is important to explore whether the information provided is accurate or a product of deception, hallucinogens, hypnosis, illusion, film, perceived spiritual evil, etc.

Perceived spiritual effects must be explored, including whether it was perceived that anything was attached to, or "captured" from, the child in this event, and whether words were spoken for spiritual control, such as claims, curses, commands, and covenants. It may be important to discover whether this event resulted in the perception of portals or astral pathways that allowed abusers continued spiritual access to the child.

Sample beginning of a dialogue to discover programming

Is there a particular event we have to look at to help this part? Yes.

Do I have permission to ask the age of the body at the time of that event? Yes.

How old was the body at the time of this event? Three.

Do I have permission to ask about the location of this event at age three? Yes.

Was this event indoors or outdoors? Indoors. In a house.

And this event in a house, was it where the body lived or another house? Another.

Do I have permission to ask whose house? No.

Do I have permission to ask who took the child to this house? Yes.

Who took the child to this house? The grandmother.

Did the grandmother dress the child for this event? Yes.

How did the grandmother dress the body? A dress.

May I ask the colour of the dress? Black. [Often a colour used for sacrifice.]

Did the child wear anything else? A chain.

Where was the chain worn? Around the waist.

Did anything hang from the chain? Yes. A locket.

Did the locket have a stone, a carving? A portrait.

Am I allowed to ask the subject of the portrait? No.

Did the grandmother place this locket on the child? No.

Am I allowed to ask who placed the locket? The lady in the portrait.

Am I allowed to know if this person was a rival of the grand-mother? Yes, she was.

When the grandmother brought the child to this event, did she present her to someone? The rival.

Did either of them speak? Yes.

May I know who spoke first? The grandmother. She said, "I give you my granddaughter."

Did the rival respond? Yes, she said, "You have done well."

At this event at three, were others present? Yes.

How many others? Twelve.

Were any male? No.

Were there other children present? Yes.

May I know how many? Three.

Were any male? One newborn baby boy.

Am I allowed to ask the ages of the two female children? Three and six.

Were these children already known to the child? Yes.

Am I allowed to know who they were? No.

Where were the other children when the body was presented to the rival? The girls were on altars. The boy was with one of the ladies.

After the rival received the child, what happened next? She was placed on the altar.

Who placed the child on the altar? The grandmother.

On an altar by herself? With the other three-year-old.

Were words spoken when the grandmother placed the body on the altar? Yes.

Am I allowed to know the words? Part.

What part may I know? "I give you to . . ."

Spoken by the grandmother? Yes.

And when she spoke those words, what happened next? . . .

This continued piecemeal, until the event was completed. Then, "disconnecting" the harm, physical, mental, spiritual, etc., culminating in rescue of the three-year-old ego state, can begin, as follows.

Resolution of programming once it is made conscious

Making programming conscious is very challenging. Resolving programming once it is made conscious is comparatively easy. It relies on defiance of programmers' directives, training, conditioning, and hypno-suggestions; assertion of one's will against abuser attempts at spiritual bondage; use of one's imaginative capacity and the malleability of the unconscious mind to re-sculpt the inner world to one's own needs and wishes; communication and negotiation with significant ego states; "rescue" of self-states from their abusers and from the sites of their torture to an inner place of healing; in some cases, integration of ego states into the self. These changes are most deeply accomplished while the survivor is still in the inner place created to do the work of discovering and resolving programming.

Svali (1996) explains that survivors can use a limitless creative capacity to overcome programming:

> The good news is that this internal landscape is highly malleable. Once parts are "found", and the binds that trap them in harmful sites are discovered and resolved, they can be helped to permanently relocate to places of safety and healing in the internal world. And scenes and structures installed in the mind to cause harm can be removed. In essence, the work of healing and disabling programming uses to the survivor's advantage what programmers used to their disadvantage: the limitless malleability of the internal landscape.

Krystal (1988) captured the essence of this therapeutic approach when he wrote about helping traumatized alexithymic patients achieve a "wish-based psychic structure" and the need for patients to be in trance-like states to modify self- and object-representations:

> The patient, formerly suffering a psychic 'hole', has to be helped (at some risk) to convert the absence of psychic representation to a wish-based psychic structure. [p. 482]

> In my extensive work on this subject, I came to the conclusion that because the problems of alexithymics are a reaction to conflicts registered as preverbal, infantile, or purely affective memories, the usual approaches of psychoanalytic psychotherapy fail us. To deal with such early and/or severe trauma, the patients have to experience trancelike states in which modifications of self- and object-representations can be achieved. [p. 481]

Conscious processing of tricks, illusions, lies, and set-ups

Once programming tricks, lies, films, set-ups, etc., are made conscious, revealed for what they are, and the affected self-states are discovered, they lose their potency. The survivor now has the conscious capacity to mentally reject the intended messages, perceptions, and set-ups. Programmed triggers come under conscious control. In some instances, triggers are further mastered by changing them to impossible stimuli, like a purple and blue polka-dotted apple playing the saxophone.

Self-states formed or harmed in these events need help to leave these scenarios. They need physical, emotional, and often spiritual, separation from the abuse they endured.

Physical separation involves guiding the survivor to use his or her spiritual source, strong and helpful ego states, powerful animals, or even inanimate devices, to "go into the memory", push the abusers back away from abused self-states, detach them from the devices of torture, cleanse their bodies of any abusive drugs, toxins, blood, sexual substances, etc., destroy the equipment (electroshock machines, restraints, film projectors), and to relocate the affected self-states to the inner place of healing. Most survivors readily employ such suggestions. Some survivors initially express that these interventions feel artificial or invalidate their abuse. I share that I agree that this work will not change that this abuse occurred, and the memory will never disappear, but that for self-states who perceive themselves "stuck" in the sites of their abuse, this "adds an additional frame" to this memory, a corrective ending, and that this ending also reflects truths, such as their love and compassion for hurt parts of themselves.

Psychological and "spiritual" separation also usually require guidance by the therapist, at least initially. Survivors have been so intimidated and dominated by the mind-set of their abusers that they initially feel unable to think outside of the abusers' frame. For example, survivors manipulated into harming others usually believe, as their abusers intended, that they are deeply evil. Therapists have the natural impulse to want to argue with survivors about their having been given no good choices, that everyone has a breaking point when tortured, that there is a survival instinct that takes over when one's life is threatened, etc. These approaches may help in the long term, but rarely have an impact short-term. The guilt is existential. And it is natural to unconsciously seek to undo harm done to others through suffering and self-punishment. I have found that a more useful immediate intervention is to guide the survivor through a pronouncement or prayer and to ask them to repeat my words if they feel that I am speaking truth, and to stop and correct me if I have it wrong. I say something like:

> I, [name], on behalf of all of my parts, refuse to submit to [abusers'] claim that I am as evil as they are. The truth is that I never wanted to do [act]. I was coerced by [abusers]. I did not do [act] of my free will. They gave me two choices that were both unbearable. It is a lie that I agreed to this act. Any agreement made under torture, threat, or trickery is invalid, legally and spiritually. I reject their statement that I was evil. That lie belongs to them, not to me. I choose the truth that I was an innocent, terrified child who deserved love, protection, and respect.

Generally, all of these steps must occur before affected self-states can be rescued to a healing place. If affected self-states are unable to be moved to a healing place, it usually signifies that critical elements of the event have not been discovered and resolved. It is helpful to ask, "Is there something else we need to know before these parts can go to your healing place?" On occasion, ego states need to "tell their stories", release their emotions and sorrow, before they can be relocated.

Conscious choice against directives, claims, curses, covenants, threats, etc.

Words that abusers and programmers pair with torture have a deep and devastating effect on their victims. It is important to reject or renounce verbal commands and proclamations, especially words to define the roles or nature of self-states, assigned names, claims of spiritual ownership or evil, curses to threaten or create expectations of harm, covenants (coerced agreements), triggers to call forward self-states, codes to access, activate, re-set, back-up, programmes, and, in many cases, to replace these in declarations or prayer with proclamations, blessings, new names, new roles and defining purposes, impossible stimuli (for triggers and codes) etc., of one's own choosing.

An anonymous survivor and psychotherapist explained the critical importance of discovering the words of programmers:

The last and very necessary step of dismantling the structure, for me, was to remember exactly what the programmer told me and the imagery that I created from this. Once I realized that the structure was that way because of what someone told me, I was able to dissolve it permanently. Strangely, just knowing that the programmer told me to make it that way did not work. I had to remember exactly what he said and what I did in response. I did not always do exactly what they wanted, but sometimes just told them I did. What I did in response to what they said was just as important as what they said for me to get rid of the structure.

Formal declarations and prayers have a powerful effect in overcoming words intended to define, control, and harm the survivor. Here is a sample prayer to rename a self-state:

I ask you God, on behalf of myself and all of my parts, to hold this three-year-old part of me and let her know in her heart that the abusers lied to her when they told her that her name was Unlovable. That was a lie. She has always been lovable. Please let her feel your love and let her feel our love. Please let her know that the abusers tried to give her that name so she would never feel worthy to reach out to anyone who would really love her. They knew that name was a lie when they said it. We never agreed to that name. I give that name back to the abusers. I ask you God to bless her with the new name of [survivor's choice, such as Sweet Little Girl].

Psychological and spiritual separation
of perceived spiritual attachments

I believe that ritually abused clients reveal their experiences of spiritual evil only to people whom they sense are receptive to its possible existence and who convey some genuine comfort in being able to help with it. Without this support, many survivors do not allow the perception of spiritual evil to become conscious. When clients perceive the presence of spiritual evil, internally or externally, I usually work with that perception, rather than initiating dialogue about whether the perceived evil is real or not. If I were to try to convince a ritually abused client that human spirits or entities are not real, to try to reduce their fear, etc., I might stand a chance with some hosts, but no chance with self-states raised in Satanism or abusive witchcraft. Those self-states were raised in cultures rooted in theologies that such entities are more powerful and enduring than human life. And these self-states are barely orientated to the outside world. Programming is most deeply resolved when it succeeds in changing the reality of programmed alters in the inner world. Whether such "evil" is spiritually real or not, it is psychologically real to these self-states, and I believe it can only be dealt with as such.

I have found that to achieve "separation" of perceived attachments, whether this mechanism is partly spiritual or only psychological, survivors must recall the rituals in which "transfers" and "captures" were perceived to be accomplished, and then assert their will to reject each act. I tell survivors that I believe that any act intended to spiritually control children, who are not aware that they had any choice to the contrary, can now be opposed and "separated" spiritually and psychologically by a simple act of one's will, that we each have control of our spiritual self. I believe that an overwhelmed, frightened, and abused psyche is what permitted the perceived "admission" of these entities and introjects. Making the trauma conscious and the exercise of free will is what allows for their rejection and separation.

Many survivors use traditionally religious approaches or personal spiritual approaches to "remove" perceived "attachments" and to retrieve "captured" parts of the self. This work generally includes the use of a spiritual base to refuse the abusers' right to have abused them, to refuse the words intended to bind them, to refuse the spirit or entity to remain, to will it to leave, to close all perceived portals, to sever all perceived astral pathways, and to declare one's right, or ask the spiritual source, to have all parts of one's self returned, with none of the abusers' spirits, words, evil, or deities/demons attached.

Technological programming can also result in the perception of "introjects" dwelling within, often intentionally "placed" by programmers. These can also be "separated" by one's will or spiritual source.

Many survivors easily differentiate self-states from perceived introjects or entities. For others, the therapist can help the survivor differentiate these through dialogue. Self-states, even those with a hostile veneer, usually desire some human connection with the therapist, are motivated to feel "better", and their hostility has a quality of underlying fear and pain. Perceived introjects and entities generally do not establish a "felt" human connection with the therapist. Instead, they demonstrate scorn for the survivor and intense hatred for the therapist.

In many cases, when the work seems "stuck", survivors may have the sense that "spiritual evil" is interfering. If they perceive that "evil" is being "sent" in the present, survivors can usually easily refuse its presence by asserting their will in intention or prayer. In the case of perceived interference by introjects or entities "attached" in prior abuse, it usually helps to "place" these in opaque, soundproof containers, guarded by spiritual protection if the survivor wishes. As the event is processed, words of control, implements and bodily substances of abuse, attached deities, etc., can also be placed in these containers. Once the event is fully processed, the container and its contents are generally easily expelled.

I have consistently observed that when affected self-states perceive spirits and entities to be gone, the survivor experiences tremendous relief. To date, no survivor I have worked with ever felt that they had separated a part of the self in the process.

"Removal" of structures

"Removal" of "structures", especially foundational structures, can be challenging, especially early in a survivor's recovery. Some structures are "placed" with near-death torture in the unconscious mind, "beneath" the self-state system. A meta-view of the inner world is often necessary to discover such structures. The programmer's goal is for the terror of death to secure the structure against any attempt to tamper with it by the victim, or by rival programmers.

Programmers often "install" structures with booby-traps to prevent their removal. Wires to explosive or electroshock devices may connect self-states and structures. Some programmers attach "demons" or "spirits" to protect their structures. A self-state may be programmed to be a loyal servant or good soldier to guard the structure. Structures may be connected and layered, more hidden

structures installed by more skilled programmers. Rival programmers often compete to control victims.

Self-states trapped within, or connected to structures, have very
little, if any, self-agency. They define themselves by the reality of the
programmers who dictated that the structures can only be removed
by their own parameters. Some programmers install a complex
series of steps that must be followed to remove a structure, including explosive devices that must first be emptied of their explosive
substances, then removed, codes to deactivate booby-traps along
the way, separation of "demons", a master erase code, and modification of re-set codes to prevent their use.

Stimuli associated with a programme installation often serve as
re-sets and must be contained, destroyed, removed, etc. Undis-
covered stimuli can later serve to re-set programming, by programme design, for example, "When you hear this song, this grid
will reappear in your chest", and by classical conditioning of associated stimuli with pain, terror, and programmer commands. It is,
therefore, helpful to check, "Was there anything else being perceived in this event?" Words, music, smells, tastes, sights, and physical sensations can be changed to "impossible stimuli". Tools of
torture must be separated from abused states, including drugs,
toxins, wires, constraints, things used to rape, body fluids (blood,
semen), "spirits", and "demons". Devices and substances can be
changed to benign objects, destroyed, or washed clean, by an act of
will or by one's spiritual source.

Programmers may initially install structures with the require-
ment that in order to remove the structure, the victim must be re-
tortured in the same way while saying the removal code,. In
actuality, this can be accomplished in imagination only and very
quickly, while the removal code is said. In doing so, it is very
important that the survivor mentally remains in the safe place
rather than "slip into" the site of the torture.

Some survivors remove structures, fundamental and otherwise,
from the inner world without following programmer "rules". This
generally requires awareness of the structure and self-states
trapped within, and development of much "true self", with compassion for what all self-states endured and forgiveness for what
they were forced into doing to others. This capacity for self-love,
setting intentions and/or spiritual faith, can be used to free self-

states from structures and to remove the structures. Many survivors report that structures only "work" if self-states connected to them perceive them as real. When the programming is made conscious, even if only in significant ISH, and the trapped self-states understand that the structure that surrounds them is only an illusion, the structure simply vanishes.

Rutz (2003) realized that creative visualization was how her programming was done and used this same capacity to erase barriers and booby-traps and to deactivate and remove structures:

> A lot of my programming revolved around the Wizard of Oz. The hourglass was used in the event I would begin to remember and talk. They would tell us that if we talked the hourglasses [sic] sand would begin to run and when it was all run out we must do ourself in. We turned the hourglass on its side so it could no longer be used to threaten us. I was also told my head would explode. When I ran into this the first time, I was driving home from therapy. My head not only felt like it was going to explode; I saw a gigantic bomb with a lit fuse. I decided that I had used visualization for helping to heal other alters and since the programming they did was done with creative visualization, I should be able to undo it in the same way. I took my fingers and snuffed the wick out—it was that simple. Knowing their lies made it so much easier to dismantle the programming . . .

> I found there were hidden parts. We took a giant eraser and internally started erasing all the lines to the boxes and triangles inside of us. We saw people coming out on stretchers, with bandages and others internally were carrying them on cots to the healing place.

> When I was having trouble even getting close to memories we found booby traps and land mines surrounding them, so that every time we got close we couldn't get past these. We visualized a giant pacman in our blood stream. He was sent on a search and destroy mission for any programs that were implanted and dangerous. When pacman was through destroying these he yelled, "Mission Accomplished." Our progress after this was remarkable.

Relocation of self-states to an inner healing place

Once released from programme controls, survivors can use their imaginative and spiritual capacity to "relocate" hurt self-states from sites of abuse and programme structures to a place of healing within.

Often, only "a part of a part" can be located to a healing place when an event has been processed, because that self-state was abused repeatedly over many events.

Some ego-states require therapeutic help before moving to a healing place. Many need their feelings and experiences honoured and witnessed. Many need to critically evaluate the agenda of their abusers, now that they can safely do so. Many must grieve perceived bonds to their abusers. Some need the protective function of their abuser loyalty to be understood. Some have intense rage, and need to develop constructive channels to release it, or to contain or dissolve it imagistically or spiritually.

For Rutz (2003), "Neverland" held a pre-verbal baby who never grew up and "Shadowland" held an alter trained as an assassin. When she tried to rescue these trapped alters, they were initially afraid to leave their familiar places. She needed to communicate with them to get them to safety:

> It took a longtime [sic] and a good deal of work, to find this and break free, since even after the alters found out the truth they did not want to leave their lands right away where they felt safe and come to the safe place in my system. After some internal communication the baby was rescued from Neverland. Alters simply created a bridge and crossed from there to Shadowland. Our baby part was nurtured by our alter who was trained for killing, so it was very beneficial to both those alters. The door to Neverland was burned and holes were shot in the ceiling of Shadowland to let light through ... eventually everyone felt safe enough so that an elevator was built to the healing place and Shadowland was destroyed too.

Ongoing spiritual, psychological, and physical healing occurs in the inner healing place. I ask clients what their self-states need for physical comfort, cleansing, love (pets are a common wish), etc. They may choose to have me ask their spiritual source to provide these, or may have ISH provide these.

There is a significant easing once ego-states are relocated to the inner healing place. It is often a full resolution for programmed fragmentary self-states. Once their programming is conscious and they have been relocated to a place of healing, they only need safety, love from the self or the survivor's spiritual source, and time to heal. They need not be actively engaged in therapy or "integrated" with the "true self" or host. More substantial ego states also require much emotional release, grieving, and sharing of experience and memory with the "true self", host, and therapist. I do not encourage integration, but view it as a very personal and seamless process that usually occurs as barriers between ego states are no longer needed.

In the process of resolving, overcoming, and removing programming, major shifts occur in self-states and in the internal landscape (inner world). This can be unsettling in that the familiar is no longer so.

When large structures that housed self-states are gone, some survivors perceive a "void". This usually must be replaced. A healing place provides a home and sense of grounding for previously programmed parts. Survivors create many other new and helpful places in their inner worlds.

Many survivors discover a foundational programme structure that separated two sides of their self-state system. The host side is amnestic for the other side, where most self-states endured very serious abuse as both victims and perpetrators. Once this barrier is gone, each side must develop compassion for the other. The host must face the horrors the abuse-bound parts endured and not recoil from them. The abuse-bound side must forgive the host for not enduring more abuse and must appreciate the host's role in living the normal side of life. Ultimately, they all must face that everyone was hurt and that they share this common bond. Survivor support groups can be of great help in resolving these conflicts.

Survivors can look forward to deeply moving changes. Rutz explains (2009, personal communication),

> Each alter's job is normal to that alter. It's all they know. Just as an abused child who is being incested and is told that is love, learns to believe that lie. They don't know any better, so to them that is "Normal." An alter like Samantha only knows pain, so why wouldn't it be normal. As I was healing, it was so vital to allow each alter to choose a new job or a new way of life. For instance, Guy chose to rock the Baby part and comfort her when the barriers between Neverland and Shadowland were dissolved. Think what

that meant to the system's healing to have a part that was a trained killer be able to feel love and give love. That was huge.

Once substantial work has been achieved, and enough parts are in the inner place of healing, the hidden "core", an early and central aspect of the self that the individual had kept long-hidden from abusers, or that the programmers had sequestered, may feel safe enough to make itself known to the "true self", host, and therapist. Other major integrations of the self-system may spontaneously occur. This often results in a sense of vitality. Senses may feel heightened. One survivor reported truly seeing colour for the first time. There is often a sense of truly being alive in the world for the first time.

References

Adams, M. A. (1989). Internal self helpers of persons with multiple personality disorder. *Dissociation*, *II*(3): 138–143.

Barber, T. X. (2000). A deeper understanding of hypnosis: its secrets, its nature, its essence. *American Journal of Clinical Hypnosis*, 42(3)/42(4), January–April: 208–272.

Beauchaine, T.P., Gatzke-Kopp, L., & Mead, H. K. (2007). Polyvagal theory and developmental psychopathology: emotion dysregulation and conduct problems from preschool to adolescence. *Biological Psychology*, 74(2): 174–184.

Becker, T., Karriker, W., Overkamp, B., & Rutz, C. (2007). *Extreme Abuse Survey Project*. Accessed 12 June 2010 at: http://extreme-abuse-survey.net http://extreme-abuse-survey.net.

Blinder, B. J. (2007). The autobiographical self: who we know and who we are. *Psychiatric Annals*, 37(4): 276–284.

Chu, J. A., Frey, L. M., Ganzel, B. L., & Matthews, J. A. (1999). Memories of childhood abuse: Dissociation, amnesia, and corroboration. *American Journal of Psychiatry*, 156(5): 749–755.

Clark, P. B. (2001). Magic surgery and the formation of the inner world. In: *Restoring Survivors of Satanic Ritual Abuse: Equipping and Releasing God's People for Spirit-Empowered Ministry* (formerly entitled, *His Presence in Abuse Counseling*). Los Angeles, CA: Bairdspong. Accessed 12 June 2010 at: www.suite101.com/print_article.cfm/ritual_abuse/71201.

Cleghorn, R. (1990). The McGill experience of Robert A. Cleghorn, MD: Recollections of D. Ewen Cameron. *Canadian Bulletin of Medical History/Bulletin canadien d'histoire de la médecine*, 7(1): 53–76. Accessed 12 June 2010 at: www.cbmh.ca/index.php/cbmh/article/view/224/223.

Collins, A. (1988). *In the Sleep Room: The Story of the CIA Brainwashing Experiments in Canada*. Toronto, Ontario: Key Porter Books.

Comstock, C. M. (1991). Inner self helper and concepts of inner guidance: historical antecedents, its role within dissociation, and clinical utilization. *Dissociation, IV*(3): 165–177.

Conway, A. (1994). Trance formations of abuse. In: V. Sinason (Ed.), *Treating Survivors of Satanist Abuse* (pp. 254–264). New York: Routledge.

Conway, F., & Siegelman, J. (2005). *Snapping: America's Epidemic of Sudden Personality Change* (2nd edn). New York: Stillpoint Press.

Dell, P. (2009). Understanding dissociation. In: P. Dell & J. O'Neil (Eds.), *Dissociation and the Dissociative Disorders: DSM-V and Beyond* (pp. 709–825). New York: Routledge.

Draijer, N., & Langeland, W. (1999). Childhood trauma and perceived parental dysfunction in the etiology of dissociative symptoms in psychiatric in-patients. *American Journal of Psychiatry, 156*(3): 379–385.

Einhorn, L. (2006). *Forgiveness and Child Abuse: Would You Forgive?* Bandon, OR: Robert Reed. Retrieved from http://mcrais.googlepages.com/emery.htm.

Fassin, V., Rechtman, R., & Gomme, R. (2009). *The Empire of Trauma: An Inquiry into the Condition of Victimhood*. Princeton, NJ: Princeton University Press.

Fotheringham, T. (2008). Patterns in mind-control: a first person account. In: J. R. Noblitt & P. S. Perskin Noblitt (Eds.), *Ritual Abuse in the Twenty-first Century: Psychological, Forensic, Social and Political Considerations* (pp. 491–540). Bandon, OR: Robert Reed.

Fox, H. (1993). Patients' fear of and objection to electroconvulsive therapy. *Hospital and Community Psychiatry, 44*: 357–360.

Frankel, A. S., & O'Hearn, T. C. (1996). Similarities in responses to extreme and unremitting stress: cultures of communities under siege. *Psychotherapy, 33*(3): 485–502.

Freeman, H. (1987). In conversation with William Sargant. *Bulletin of the Royal College of Psychiatrists, 11*(September): 290–294. Accessed 14 April 2010 at: http://pb.rcpsych.org/cgi/reprint/11/9/290.pdf.

Goulding, R., & Schwartz, R. (1995). *The Mosaic Mind: Empowering the Tormented Selves of Child Abuse Survivors*. New York: Norton.

Gresch, H. U. (2010). *Hypnose Bewusstseinskontrolle Manipulation: Bewusstseinskontrolle durch Persönlichkeitsspaltung*. Dusseldorf: Elitär Verlag.

Hauff, W. (1858). *Das kalte Herz* (The cold heart). Lexington, MA:: D. C. Heath. Accessed 14 April 2010 at: www.sanmayce.com/The%20Cold%20Heart/WILHELM%20HAUFF%20-%20THE%20COLD%20HEART_1.pdf.

Heim, A. (1892). Notizen uber den Tod durch absturz (Remarks on fatal falls). *Jahrbuch des Schweizer Alpenclub*, 27: 327–337. Translated and reprinted in English as R. Noyes & R. Kletti (1980). The experience of dying from falls. In: R. A. Kalish (Ed.), *Death, Dying, Transcending* (pp. 129–136). Farmingdale, NY: Baywood.

Kernberg, O. F. (1994). Aggression, trauma, and hatred in the treatment of borderline patients. *Psychiatric Clinics of North America*, 17(4): 701–714.

Krystal, H. (1988). On some roots of creativity. *Psychiatric Clinics of North America*, 11(3): 475–491.

Lacter, E., & Lehman, K. (2008). Guidelines to differential diagnosis between schizophrenia and ritual abuse/mind control traumatic stress. In: J. R. Noblitt & P. Perskin Noblitt (Eds.), *Ritual Abuse in the Twenty-first Century: Psychological, Forensic, Social and Political Considerations* (pp. 85–154). Bandon, OR: Robert Reed.

LeDoux, J. (1996). *The Emotional Brain: The Mysterious Underpinnings of Emotional Life*. New York: Simon and Schuster.

LeDoux, J. (2007). Emotional memory. *Scholarpedia*, 2(7): 1806, revision #38756. Accessed 12 June 2010 at: www.scholarpedia.org/article/Emotional_memory doi:10.4249/scholarpedia.1806.

Lezak, M. (1995). *Neuropsychological Assessment* (3rd edn). New York: Oxford University Press.

Marks, J. (1979). *The Search for the Manchurian Candidate: The CIA and Mind Control: The Secret History of the Behavioral Sciences*. New York: Norton.

McGonigle, H. L. (1999). A look at the law and government mind control through five cases. Accessed 12 June 2010 at: http://ritual-abuse.us/mindcontrol/articles-books/the-law-and-mind-control-a-look-at-the-law-and-goverment-mind-control-through-five-cases/.

Miller, A. (2008). Recognizing and treating survivors of abuse by organized criminal groups. In: J. R. Noblitt & P. Perskin Noblitt (Eds.),

Ritual Abuse in the Twenty-first Century: Psychological, Forensic, Social and Political Considerations (pp. 443–477). Bandon, OR: Robert Reed.

MKULTRA declassified documents archive: http://abuse-of-power. org/modules/content/index.php?id=31.

MKULTRA declassified document (3 December 1951). Artichoke [redacted] (MORI ID 146342). Accessed 12 June 2010 at: http:// abuse-of-power.org/modules/content/index.php?id=31:

MKULTRA declassified document (January 25, 1952). Memorandum for: Chief, Medical Staff Subject: PROJECT ARTICHOKE, Evaluation of ISSO Role (MORI ID 144686). Accessed 12 June 2010 at: http://abuse-of-power.org/modules/content/index.php?id=31.

MKULTRA declassified document (10 February 1954). Subject: hypnotic experimentation and research (MORI ID 190691). Accessed 12 June 2010 at: http://abuse-of-power.org/modules/ content/index.php?id=31.

MKULTRA declassified document (5 May 1955). Hypnotism and covert operations. (MORI ID 190713). Accessed 12 June 2010 at: http:// abuse-of-power.org/modules/content/index.php?id=31.

MKULTRA declassified document (1955, 1956, 1957). *Studies of Dissociated States, of Sub-project 43 and Psychophysiological Studies of Hypnosis and Suggestibility (1956)* (MORI ID 017441). Accessed 12 June 2010 at: http://abuse-of-power.org/modules/content/index. php?id=31.

MKULTRA declassified document (23 August 1961). Memorandum for the Record, Subject: Project MKULTRA, Subproject 136 (MORI ID 017395). Accessed 12 June 2010 at: http://abuse-of-power.org/ modules/content/index.php?id=31http://michael-robinett. com/declass/c000.htm (p. 1).

Neutra, W. (1920). *Seelenmechanik und Hysterie* (Mechanics of the Soul and Hysteria). Leipzig: Vogel.

Nichols, M., & Schwartz, R. (1991). *Family Therapy; Concepts and Methods*. Boston, MA: Allyn & Bacon.

Nijenhuis, E. R. S., & den Boer, J. A. (2007). Psychobiology of traumatization and trauma-related structural dissociation of the personality. In: E. Vermettern, M. Dorahy, & D. Spiegel (Eds.), *Traumatic Dissociation: Neurobiology and Treatment* (pp. 202–218). Washington, DC: American Psychiatric Association.

Ogawa, J. R., Sroufe, A., Weinfield, N. S., Carlson, E. A., & Egeland, B. (1997). Development and the fragmented self: longitudinal study of dissociative symptomatology in a nonclinical sample. *Development and Psychopathology, 9*: 855–879.

Parker, E. S., Cahill, L., & McGaugh, J. L. (2006). A case of unusual auto-biographical remembering. *Neurocase, 12*(1): 35–49.

Pavlov, I. P. (1941). *Conditioned Reflexes and Psychiatry, Volume 2 of Lectures on Conditioned Reflexes.* Introduction by W. H. Gantt. New York: International Universities Press.

Peterson, G. (1991). Children coping with trauma: diagnosis of "dissociation identity disorder". *Dissociation Progress in the Dissociative Disorders, 4*(3): 152–164.

Porges, S. W. (1995). Orienting in a defensive world: mammalian modifications of our evolutionary heritage. A polyvagal theory. *Psychophysiology,* 32: 301–318.

Porges, S. W. (1999). Emotion: an evolutionary by-product of the neural regulation of the autonomic nervous system. In: C. S. Carter, B. Kirkpatrick, & I. I. Lederhendler (Eds.), *The Integrative Neurobiology of Affiliation, Annals of the New York Academy of Sciences* (pp. 65–80). Cambridge, MA: MIT Press.

Project MKULTRA, the CIA's Program of Research into Behavioral Modification. Joint Hearing before the Select Committee on Intelligence and the Subcommittee on Health and Scientific Research of the Committee on Human Resources, United State Senate, Ninety-Fifth Congress, First Session. (1977). US Government Printing Office (copy hosted at the *New York Times* website). Accessed 12 June 2010 at: www.nytimes.com/packages/pdf/national/13inmate_ProjectMKULTRA.pdf.

Putnam, F. W. (1997). *Dissociation in Children and Adolescents: A Developmental Perspective.* New York: Guilford Press.

Putnam, F. W., & Carlson, E. B. (2002). Hypnosis, dissociation, and trauma: myths, metaphors, and mechanisms . In: D. Bremner & C. Marmar (Eds.), *Trauma, Memory, and Dissociation* (pp. 27–55). Washington, DC: American Psychiatric Press.

Pynoos, R. S., Steinberg, A. M., & Goenjian, A. (1996). Traumatic stress in childhood and adolescence: recent developments and current controversies. In: B. A. van der Kolk, A. C. McFarlane, & L. Weisaeth (Eds.), *Traumatic Stress: The Effects of Overwhelming Experience on Mind, Body, and Society* (pp. 331–358). New York: Guilford Press.

Rejali, D. (2009). *Torture and Democracy.* Princeton, NJ: Princeton University Press.

Ross, C. A. (1995). *Satanic Ritual Abuse: Principles of Treatment.* Toronto: University of Toronto Press.

Ross, C. (2000). *Bluebird: Deliberate Creation of Multiple Personality by Psychiatrists*. Richardson, TX: Manitou Communications.

Rutz, C. (2001). *A Nation Betrayed*. Grass Lake, MI: Fidelity.

Rutz, C. (2003). Healing from ritual abuse and mind control, a Presentation to the Sixth Annual Ritual Abuse, Secretive Organizations and Mind Control Conference, 8–10 August. Accessed 12 June 2010 at: http://ritualabuse.us/smart-conference/conf03/healing-from-ritual-abuse-and-mind-control/.

Sargant, W. (1957). *Battle for the Mind: A Physiology of Conversion and Brain-washing*. London: Heinemann.

Scheflin, A. W., & Opton, E. M. (1978). *The Mind Manipulators*. New York: Paddington Press. Retrieved from http://www.lynnsart.net/.

Schwartz, H. (2000). *Dialogues with Forgotten Voices: Relational Perspectives on Child Abuse Trauma and the Treatment of Severe Dissociative Disorders*. New York: Basic Books.

Shorter, E., & Healy, D. (2007). *History of Electroconvulsive Treatment in Mental Illness*. New Brunswick: Rutgers University Press.

Steele, K., van der Hart, O., & Nijenhuis, E. (2009). The theory of trauma-related structural dissociation of the personality. In: P. Dell & J. O'Neil (Eds.), *Dissociation and the Dissociative Disorders: DSM-V and Beyond* (pp. 239–258). New York: Routledge.

Svali (1996). How the cult programs people. Accessed 12 June 2010 at: http://www.bibliotecapleyades.net/sociopolitica/esp_sociopol_illuminati_svali01a.htm; http://www.mindcontrolforums.com/svali_speaks.htm.

Tammet, D. (2007). *Born on a Blue Day: Inside the Extraordinary Mind of an Autistic Savant*. New York: Free Press.

Thomas, G. (1989). *Journey Into Madness: The True Story of Secret CIA Mind Control and Medical Abuse*. New York: Bantam.

Thomas, G. (1998). Memorandum to Eric Olson, 30th November 1998. Accessed 12 June 2010 at: www.frankolsonproject.org/Statements/Statement-G.Thomas.html.

Thompson, G. (2004). *The Ethic of Honesty: The Fundamental Rule of Psychoanalysis*. Amsterdam: Rodopi.

Tien, H. C. (1974). 100 questions and answers on ELT: the electrolytic therapy of psychosynthesis. *World Journal of Psychosynthesis, 6*: 31–39.

van der Hart, O., Nijenhuis, E. R. S., & Steele, K. (2006). *The Haunted Self: Structural Dissociation and the Treatment of Chronic Traumatization*. New York: Norton.

van der Kolk, B. A. (1989). The compulsion to repeat the trauma: re-enactment, revictimization, and masochism. *Psychiatric Clinics of North America, 12*(2): 389–411.

van der Kolk, B. A., McFarlane, A. C., & Weisaeth, L. (Eds.) (1996). *Traumatic Stress: The Effects of Overwhelming Experience on Mind, Body, and Society.* New York: Guilford Press.

Watkins, J. G. (1971). The affect bridge: a hypnoanalytic technique. *International Journal of Clinical & Experimental Hypnosis, 19*: 21–27.

Watkins, J. G. (1992). *Hypnoanalytic Techniques: The Practice of Clinical Hypnosis* (Volume 2). New York: Irvington.

Weinstein, H. (1988). *Father, Son and CIA.* Halifax, Nova Scotia: Formac.

CHAPTER FOUR

Love is my religion

*Anonymous**

I was born the first daughter in a long line of first daughters. My mother came from a long line of people who took part in ritual abuse. For a long time, this was something that my father knew nothing about because this was something that happened through the women in my family, a very powerful, matriarchal family that I grew up in. I'm second generation Irish. My parents were staunch Catholics, so I was initially brought up with two ideologies—the catholic ideology and an inversion of that, which was Satanism.

My very early memories are of being a small baby in a room with my mother, grandmother, and other women; later, men joined in too, and they would cut marks on my body and they would throw me to each other, around the room. My early memories of these experiences are of being very startled, terrified, and disorientated. It was not long before I went from being one baby to two babies, three babies, more . . .

---

* Due to the libel laws in the UK and the wish to protect myself and my family, this piece is written anonymously.

The women in my family had some very twisted ideas about men and women. Men were very stupid. Women were much more powerful, much more significant, and much more important. Sex was dirty and sinful, but it was our job to satisfy men because they were weak. You had to keep them happy.

I remember being a small baby and being sexually stimulated. My body was being prepared for the things that were going to be happening to me later. I was also trained from a very young age to tolerate extreme pain and trained to dissociate, so that I left my body.

I was taken to church from a young age and made to sexually service the local priest. It was very confusing trying to make sense of the fact that we were sinners yet we were expected to provide sexual relief to priests.

When I was three years old, my mother met a man; I will call him X. My first memory of meeting X was when he came into a room, picked me up by my hair, and started swinging me around, and everybody laughed because when he put me down I was really dizzy. He would switch between being incredibly cruel and frightening to being very, very, charming, and a lot of my experiences were about trying to please him and trying to get on to the charming side of him. My mother became involved with X. He used her to get to me and to other children in my family. She had already been abusing me from birth, not just in a ritual situation, but also at home. There was a part of her that would lose control and she would bare her teeth and her eyes would light up and she would become crazed. She would do things like pick me up by my hair and put me in the washing machine. So just being at home is a trigger, there are so many triggers in the environment. I'm at home with my kids and I put the washing machine on and suddenly I am there, drowning, spinning, choking.

So, although my mother was already a very frightening woman by the time I was three, meeting this man and the sort of world that he inhabited meant the abuse was taken to a whole other level. One of my earliest memories of her with him is being taken to a forest and being taken into this small room; I don't know what it was, I was very small and I was disorientated. I am tied to a table and a man I have never seen starts putting electric shocks through my feet and on my genitals, before sexually abusing me. I am just screaming and screaming and screaming and then my mother comes in with X. They look like they'd probably just had sex or something, they've got their arms wrapped around each other and they just stand over me and they laugh. I'm just pleading, mummy, mummy, mummy, but she's laughing. The message was very strong—he's the person that I'm attached to, I care much more about him than you. I'd not really experienced this kind of betrayal in that way with her before. So that was the start of an established pattern of her betraying us. Of course, what he did was use that to his advantage, which I think was very deliberate on his part. He would get her to betray me then he'd take me aside and say, look at what a witch your mother is, look at how much she doesn't love you. I think you are beautiful, I think that you are a really special girl and I think that your mother is really, really stupid for not seeing what a beautiful and special girl you are. That's what he did a lot of, manipulating me, luring me in, seducing me, making me feel important in a way that I never had before. That combined with how terrified I was of him was a pretty lethal combination.

He was a performer and we would travel around to places in the UK, and I was also taken abroad. These were special shows and I remember one of many shows that I was involved with, which was in Amsterdam. It starts with a woman coming on stage. She is topless and she squeezes her breasts and squirts the audience with breast milk and everyone is delighted and laughs and then she starts to cut herself and do things like this to herself on stage. I had been primed—I was probably about eight at this time—to have sex with a boy who was around the same age as me, who was absolutely petrified. He wasn't really used to this stuff in the way that I was by this point. So I had to tell him before we went on what we were going to do. I explained to him, I'm going to do this to you, and then you do that to me, and so on. We then go on stage and the audience clearly get off on it.

X's big thing, his speciality, was creating parts. What he liked to believe was that he was giving birth to these different parts—creating new souls. He would call himself a Gnostic, which is allegedly a synthesis of a lot of different belief systems, different religious beliefs, mythological beliefs, philosophical beliefs: Christianity, Judaism, Hinduism, Buddhism, Tantra, sex magick, Paganism, alchemy, worshipping innumerable deities, gods and goddesses, the list goes on. Anything was up for grabs. It was a very elaborate system that he created within me. It was based on the kabbalah, the tree of life, and the tarot, and what was sold to me was this idea that I was the chosen one, that I was very special and very fortunate to inhabit this world. He ensured that we underwent a very vigorous training, which involved things like going to a master of kundalini yoga. From a very young age we were trained to read esoteric texts, sit in extreme yoga postures for hours on end, to meditate, to chant. I believed very much in the things that he was telling me. We would be sitting there in these extreme yoga postures and doing all of these kinds of breathing techniques with a mask on that had nails in it. There were different things that we were doing in order to separate our minds from our bodies, getting used to experiencing extreme pain without reacting to it and awakening these different states of consciousness and different kinds of energies; he had a belief in these different kinds of energy systems based on the truth that we do have different kinds of energetic systems within our bodies. The belief in kundalini is that we have this snake that we awaken through spiritual and physical practice and we become enlightened, and, of course, he would help it along by using things like electric shocks and other torture techniques like isolation and starving to arouse this serpent that allegedly lived in my spine.

The thing that has caused me the most difficulties is these different parts that he created. Because what he essentially did was create parts that were completely dedicated to him. We were made to betray each other, for him. So, when I started to remember it, it was absolutely abhorrent to discover that there were parts of me that loved him, that loved this monster and wanted to go back to him, and would do anything for him and did do many terrible things for him. That realization was devastating to come to terms with. What part of me wanted to do was literally to cut those parts off and say well, go on, go back to him if that's what you want. But, of course, we all inhabit one body and it was not possible to do that.

He also created parts of me that would kill themselves, each other, other people, parts that were programmed to go back and kill him—if you go back to kill him, then he has got you. There was a whole system designed with particular things in mind. What he would do, for example, was starve you, spin you for hours, play loud frequency sounds, tie you to a chair, and he then might use electric shocks, until he saw that your mind had snapped and he would see that you had vacated your body, and then he would say, your name is now this. He would name this new part of me and say, you are an Egyptian goddess and your life is dedicated to death and destruction, and there would be a ritual where people would dress up and people would be chanting and they would burn things. Initially, as part of my conditioning and programming, I was taught how to kill animals and how to torture other children and then, later, much worse things.

This was a whole system and a lot of effort was put into creating it. It felt like colonizing the world—the significance of numbers, magick numbers, dangerous numbers, dates in the calendar . . . the whole world controls you. The number three is significant because if you spilt one you have two, and $1 + 2 = 3$, so that everything adds up and has this power that is inescapable. If you are colonizing all of these religions, then there is a religious festival all of the time, there is always something to celebrate and you are just bound in this world within this structure and belief system. He would have a part that was very frightened, and then he'd get another part to betray that part, and that has been another devastating thing, to try to reconcile the parts that betrayed each other. He'd call out a part (snap fingers)—that was one way he'd trigger a part and get her out that way—or he'd ring a bell, a certain sound, a different part of the body that he would hurt, so literally it was like colonizing my body. He carved and burned diagrams on my body. The left leg would connect to certain parts, for example, and he would focus on that part of me when he was torturing me and then that part of me would be associated with that part of my body. He would then be able to call that part out and say to that part, "What has she been saying?", and he's got that part to squeal on other parts. They might say, "She's a bit frightened of you." And he would say, "Oh is she now—what exactly is she frightened of?" "She doesn't like it when you do this." So he'd use that: "So and so is telling me . . ." It felt as if he chased me through my own mind. There was no escape from him. I'd literally be tied to a chair and he'd call different parts out and he would get them to verify stories by asking, "Is what she is saying true, is this what happened?" He would be doing things like sending me off on missions and he needed to know exactly what had been going on. So, for example, he was involved with freemasons and people who were quite powerful, and he would use me as a lure. I had been trained in sado-masochistic sex, so as a child I'd go to hotels to meet men that he would have arranged and I would go to the hotel room and I would do this stuff with these men and they would film it. They would have secret cameras and they would film it and then they would use that to blackmail the person in the room. Afterwards, he would be saying, "What did he say then?", if there were things that they couldn't see or hear on the camera, and he would then call out the different parts to verify this. We were used as prostitutes, we were used in pornography, we were used in these different kinds of shows and, of course, rituals.

From the ages of 7–12, this was a lot of my world. All of the time he was saying to me, your parents are idiots, they don't know how beautiful you are, so increasingly I began to feel, well, actually, I am superior to my parents. I was working my way up, I was good at this stuff. For the first time in my life, somebody was giving me really positive attention and I'd never ever had it and I felt very, very powerful. So those parts of me that were very attached to him thought my parents were really stupid and thought that the rest of the world was really stupid. We are far better, we inhabit this world where really exciting things happen, we are superior beings—it's not this normal shit that everyone else has to deal with. We inhabit this world where it's powerful and its magickal and it's really special and, of course, you are having these intense and very overwhelming experiences, particularly around sex, and a lot of how he controlled me was through my sexuality. As a baby I had already been prepared physically for sex, and remembering this stuff, for the parts of me that had no memory of the abuse, it was very disturbing to encounter these very sexualized children because it contradicted everything I'd believed about children and what children were capable of.

There were eight-year-old parts of me who were very sophisticated sexually and knew how to seduce men, who would dress up and lure men. For him, it was all about inverting and subverting things. He would get me to do these really wild things and adults would be shocked. What he was proving to them was "Look how wild and special we are, how wild children can be, that children want to be fucked, that's what children want". It was all about trying to lure people in—that's what he was trying to do. He managed to lure my father in. They lure people in and then they find out what turns people on, what their weaknesses are, and then once you are in it's hard to get back out again—you've crossed a line. And then you have to cross more lines and more lines until there is no way back out again. You move from being a victim to a perpetrator, so there is no way that you can ever tell.

The first murder of a child that I consciously remember was when I was about four or five years old. My mother was impregnated by X. My father wasn't on the scene at this point. We were taken to a big stately home; it was in the middle of summer, a big festival. She was induced the night before. So, on the Friday night, there was a ritual which was followed by an orgy which involved many people who were dressed up in costumes, cavorting in this huge room—Bacchus was one of the gods that he revered. The next day we went outside into these huge grounds. There were probably about 100 people there, so it was a big ritual, lots of people involved, and my mother is lying on the ground and X is chanting and my mother is screaming—she is in labour. I remember feeling very worried and frightened for her. She's clearly in pain, she is in the second stages of labour and she is pushing and crying and I remember thinking, poor mummy, mummy is naked with her legs open on the floor and everyone can see her, poor mummy. So a young part of me would have been out then, and then he calls somebody else out and we have to go over; she's lying on the ground with her legs open and he says, "Lick her", so we have to get on the floor and start licking her as she is in labour. The child is born, a little girl, and he places a knife in my left hand and he says things over this child, and then he puts his hand over mine and we pull the knife down the baby's chest and we kill her. He pulls her heart out and he holds it up and everybody screams and cheers and goes wild, and then this child is dismembered and consumed. I had seen things happen to babies before, but this was the first thing that I was directly involved in. I was witness to lots of things like that. I saw women having abortions performed on them, I saw women giving birth, and babies being killed and destroyed.

When I'm twelve he starts monitoring my menstrual cycle, and one day he says to me, "My darling girl, something fantastic is going to happen, you are going to have a baby." I remember thinking, well, I didn't have words, I just felt, oh. My mind could not actually envisage what he meant. It was incomprehensible.

I cross the road, as he literally lives across the road from my house, and go home. I am very frightened: the reality that at twelve years old I am pregnant—what can this mean? My mind cannot actually envisage what it means, I can't really go there. In desperation, I go to my mother and say, "Mummy, X has told me that I am going to have a baby." She looks stunned and then she goes absolutely berserk. She slaps my face and says, "You stupid, stupid bitch", and then she goes wild. There is a part of me that thinks, well, actually, you are the stupid bitch, you are the one who got me involved in all of this shit in the first place. And another part agrees that I am a stupid bitch—sex leads to pregnancy, you dirty bitch— what did you think would happen? Another part of me thinks that she is just jealous as I am his special girl, I am her greatest rival, I have surpassed her. I also know she is frightened. X is much more powerful and influential in my life than she or my father is. He is also much more terrifying—he can do whatever he likes and no one can stop him.

So, I'm pregnant, I'm twelve, I then turn thirteen and I inhabit this world where I go to school and, because I have all of these parts, I'm not pregnant while I am at school, I'm just at school. He has trained me to keep the two worlds very separate. I remember this experience of being in school in a science lesson when suddenly I feel this flutter and know it's a baby and feeling my mind just splitting in two in the science classroom at school. These worlds are starting to collide for me, these very separate worlds that I inhabit. A lot of the time when I'm not with him, I don't think about the fact that I'm pregnant, I'm not even really aware of it, and if I am, it's just too awful to contemplate. Apart from sometimes when I am in bed at night and I feel the baby moving and I have these fantasies about this baby that I'm going to have and it's going to be lovely, it's going to be perfect, and me and X are going to have this little house, and I develop this fantasy world. Of course, this isn't what is going to happen. And then I go back to the world with him and he loves the fact that I am pregnant and he makes full use of it. He arranges photo sessions where I dress up as a schoolgirl and I expose my pregnant belly and prance about and men take photos of me.

There comes a point when I know that they are going to want this baby. I know this in my heart of hearts. He turns up one day and he takes me to this flat with three other men. He's been away, so I am angry with him. Bear in mind that there are parts of me that are terribly attached to him. I say to him, "You've been away, where have you been, you left me, where have you been?" And he says, "I am back now and you know it is time now, you know what we are going to have to do." He gets a knitting needle and he sticks it inside me to induce labour and then he has sex with me, and then I have to have sex with these men, in this flat, and then he takes me to another place, because, of course, it is going to be a ritual which a lot of people will want to attend.

The process of being pregnant and giving birth involves several different parts of me; different parts of me have different experiences. I remember being in labour and I remember a part of me that's just holding on to this child, not wanting to give birth, and then another part takes over and says, get this thing out of me. I am standing in a circle surrounded by lots of people who are watching and I am holding on to X and he has sex with me in the middle of the circle and then I fall to my knees and I give birth to the child. A boy.

They take him away and they take me into this room and a doctor comes in, they say he is a doctor and he comes and examines me and he says leave her alone for a while, so they leave me alone in this room. So, essentially, I am in this room, having given birth to this child, knowing what is going to happen, and then X comes in and he says to me, "You are my special girl, you did brilliantly, come with me." He takes me into this beautiful room which has a four-poster bed and lots of candles and he takes me into bed and then he brings the baby in. We spend a night with the baby, just holding him, and I become very attached to this beautiful, precious boy. The next day X says to me, "You know that we are going to have to take him from you." They take him from me and I become hysterical. They give me an injection to calm me down and then they prepare me—put make-up on me, dress me up, and call out another part out. I walk into this room, knowing that this is when they are going to kill him. As I turn into the room I see X sitting in a throne next to my mother, who is breastfeeding my child. I begin screaming.

The child is killed and then there is a bloodbath as X cuts him into pieces. All I remember is blood, blood, blood. I am still bleeding profusely because I have just given birth, and of course the baby's blood is splattered everywhere—how could such a tiny body hold so much blood?—and then they tie me to a cross. They turn the cross upside down so that I am hanging upside down tied to the cross. Everyone is running around and screaming, elated, wild, it's a celebration after all—it is Good Friday. I'm hanging upside down on this cross with blood streaming out of me, wild and crazed, and I feel like such an idiot, such a fool. I hate myself, I hate all of them, but I am no better than them. I hate everyone and everything. That part of me often wants to go out on a killing rampage, to go out with a machine gun and just blow people up.

That was the beginning of the end for me. That experience was just too much. I started breaking down, I started not being able to function because it had all become too much to bear. X completed the programming. He had an ECT machine, which he then used to scramble my mind. He was trying to cover his tracks.

We move house to a different area. My parents very much want to get me away from X because they have lost me to him and they are terrified of him. My father has been implicated, other members of my family have been implicated, so we move. I start to forget what has happened. It's aided by my mother saying things like, "You had a happy childhood, me and daddy never hit you", and there was a part of me that just wanted to believe that. I always wanted a happy childhood.

Then, one day, I am coming back from school. I am fifteen by this time. I walk through the park; I need to go to the loo as I often do, so I go into these toilets. Suddenly, this man comes in behind me. He locks the door, throws me on the floor, and as he is slamming my head against the stone floor he says to me, "We are watching you, we know where you are, we watch you everywhere you go and if you ever speak to anyone about this we will kill you, we kill your children, we will kill anyone or anything that you ever love." Then he rapes me on the floor. Afterwards, he gets up and walks out and I just get up, I've got my knickers in my hand and I run all the way home. I never tell a soul about it because there is no one to tell.

That is the beginning of my forgetting. There was a growing mist that just descended over my whole childhood with this pervading sense of intense shame and terror that I carried around with me and a cacophony of voices in my head. I had lots of issues around eating, sleeping, and self-harm, and lots of experiences of feeling unreal, as if I was disembodied or as if I were in a bubble, separated from the rest of the world, in my own, sealed-off universe. All of these things I kept very private. I was quite petrified of both of my parents, especially my mother. The unnatural feelings that I had about my parents only served to prove that there was something inherently wrong with me.

I start to remember it again, ten years later, when I am twenty-five. I have my first daughter and it all comes flooding back to me. When I become a mother, I start hearing voices that I'd never heard before telling me that somebody is going to kill me, that somebody is going to kill my daughter, and I start having these awful visions. I would be changing my daughter's nappy and suddenly she'd be covered in blood. I started visualizing all of these things and I felt as if I was going mad. I began experiencing pain in my body, and marks and bruises appeared on my body like stigmata.

I was very fortunate, because prior to becoming pregnant I had been working with a counsellor for a couple of years, and then when I was pregnant I stopped working with him. It later proved useful that he had a sense of me as not being mad and he believed in me and he later said to me that he'd always felt that something really awful and chilling had happened to me but that he didn't know what it was. At that time, I didn't know what it was either.

After I had given birth and I started feeling as if I was going completely crazy, I went back to see him and I said to him, "I feel like I am going mad, something is happening." And he said, "Do you want to start working together again?", so that's what we did, we started working together again and then I started remembering.

I started having dreams about the street that I grew up in and things happening to me, abuse happening to me. Then one night this new voice came and said to me, 'Terrible things have happened to you and we are going to tell you what happened." And that's basically what happened. That new part of me came that had a lot of information. I didn't realize at that point that I was multiple. I knew there was something profoundly wrong with me, but I couldn't conceptualize it. That was the start of a journey that continues to this day.

I have given you something of a linear story, but this isn't how I remembered it, of course. It came back in fragments and in lots of different ways. It has come back a lot through my body, through voices, visions, and the remembering process for me has been about trying to associate and process highly dissociated experiences. I might remember things in my body and be dreaming about things or seeing things and I will be feeling sick and terrified. I don't necessarily realize that those things are connected and that they have come back to me in bits, but I've been very fortunate because there are parts of me that have really aided this process by telling me what's going on, saying that part of you is holding the body memories and another part of you has the intellectual knowledge, so get those two to talk to each other. This process is what is helping me to become whole.

Despite encountering outright denial from the many professionals that I have tried to disclose my abuse to, I have been very fortunate to encounter other brave souls who have had the courage to bear witness to my experiences. With their love and support I have been engaged for many years in a long, arduous process of truth and reconciliation, of listening and bearing witness to the horrors of my past. I have no doubt that therapy saved my life. Alongside this gruelling work, I have developed a successful career. I have become a woman on a mission of her own making. I have mothered two magnificent children who continue to teach me so much about what it means to be human. Despite having a loving, non-abusive mother, they, too, have been shaken to the core by the reverberations from my past. It will take many generations before the trauma that I have endured can be fully resolved—alas, I have learnt that I am not omnipotent!—but, as my eldest daughter said to me recently, "You have stopped the cycle, Mummy." That is my greatest achievement.

I have learnt many things on my journey: that if we forget or deny the past we are condemned to repeat it, that only the truth will set us free, and that the most powerful force, the only force that can save us in the face of such horror and destruction is LOVE. I cannot be a religious person, but love is my religion. Love is what I believe in. The greatest truth is love.

CHAPTER FIVE

Working with the Incredible Hulk

Orit Badouk Epstein

I t is a known fact that working with survivors of ritual abuse mainly involves working with female survivors. Less has been said about working with male survivors. I am going to tell you about some of my experiences with a male survivor of ritual abuse. My client, a twenty-eight-year old, very intelligent and highly creative young man, came to see me after spending most of his adult life wandering from AA to SLA (Sex, Love Anonymous) trying to combat his addiction to alcohol and watching pornography on the Internet and making calls to phone sex lines.

I will name him Bruce, after the character from the film *The Hulk*, and later on I will explain the link. Bruce was born into an upper middle-class, well-educated family (his maternal grandfather went to Oxbridge, and paternal grandmother was from the aristocracy). He grew up in a wealthy village where the golf and rugby clubs were the hub of a well-established and well-connected paedophile ring. It was in this leafy rural setting that the most horrific childhood sexual and physical abuse and mind control took place, concealed within a middle-class environment more closely associated with cream teas, Christmas parties, and sporting activities that enhanced their masculinity and superiority. These people were well connected, with access to finance, weapons, factories, mansions, and even aircraft.

From birth, Bruce was exposed to torture, abuse, and ritual rape by his parents and extended family, teachers, and a paedophile ring. He experienced child prostitution in England and abroad, as well as methods of severe abuse such as regular thumping on the head, being spun in a washing machine, being buried alive, confined in closed spaces covered with insects and snakes, made to eat faeces, terrorized by people in frightening masks and crocodile heads, forced to being electrocuted with a head device, hung off the top of a building, being put on the roof of a speeding car, being pushed out of an aeroplane, and even strapped to the wing of a flying plane. On coming to see me, Bruce displayed symptoms of severe phobias around heights, speed, reptiles, and insects, hair loss, washing in a bath, and much more. He also developed ME, severe headaches, and insomnia, all of which have now subsided in their extent.

In spite of it all, and with the help of the incredible survival mechanism we call dissociation, this brave young man had not lost touch with his creative parts. He managed to graduate from university and later on to take a second degree in media studies, but at the cost of a final breakdown. He managed to find enough resourcefulness to get into the Maytree, a respite home for the suicidal. When he got there, Bruce remembered how when he stared at his reflection in the mirror, he saw a dead person with no soul. Later, looking at the forms he had filled in at the Maytree, he was asked why he wrote that every time he has sex he felt suicidal. It was at that point that the past started flashing back into his consciousness. Although Bruce had a clear memory of his father sexually abusing him, his childhood was highly dissociated and later was displaced by alcoholism. After leaving the Maytree, he started seeing an art therapist, who was helpful but was not familiar enough with this level of trauma.

As clinicians, we all know that with this level of abuse, torture, and suffering, MPD, DID, and post trauma stress disorder (PTSD) are almost inevitable conditions. I have been working with Bruce for just over a year now. During this period, we have kept in daily contact through phone and e-mails. Our meetings take place three times a week, sometimes four. The MPD he displays is still work in progress, as the part-fragmented identities still keep on flooding into the sessions. Figure 1 is a diagram of all the personalities that have so far surfaced.

Unlike some other survivors with MPD, Bruce's part-selves were not named before therapy, but during therapy. Once we identifed the part and his characters, Bruce would often go home choosing a suitable name for that part.

I will focus only on one part-self that was instrumental in Bruce's survival, but which, unfortunately, I felt less and less safe being alone with in my consulting room. Consequently, it was crucial for me to find a rapid and effective way of working safely in order to allow our therapeutic alliance to blossom in a trusting manner.

What is attachment-based psychotherapy, and how does it work? I am afraid I do not have enough time for all the wonderful quotations I could offer. In a nutshell, attachment therapy offers a relationship that is authentic, empathic, secure, attuned, and intimate. The concept of intimacy combines a number of human needs and capacities: openness, transparency, close proximity, and the

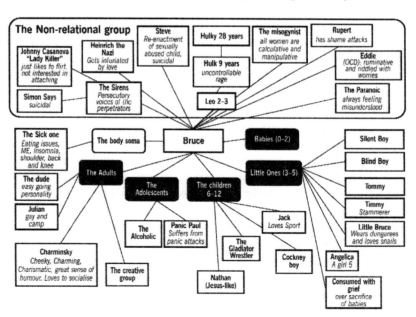

Figure 1.   Bruce's internal structure.

most important need of all is SAFETY. Something we all need, some-thing we are all entitled to when we first enter this world. We now have enough evidence to show that without such relationships, life can become a hardship with a burden of depression and illnesses.

Unfortunately, survivors of ritual abuse are robbed of their needs from birth. Not one of Bruce's basic needs was adequately met. On top of the sexual and physical abuse Bruce regularly received from his mother, father, grandmother, grandfather, and the cult, he also endured endless humiliations, mockery, and bullying that left him feeling paranoid, shamed, and guilty, feeling that it was entirely his fault, which would often trigger voices saying: "You'll go to hell, you pervert, dirty homosexual, good for noth-ing", especially around the satanic dates. Currently, Bruce and I are still fighting off these voices that seem to be an almost predictable backlash to the good progress Bruce is continuously making.

Committed and determined to get better and never missing a session, Bruce spent most of the first nine months in therapy regressing into trance states, reliving and remembering his horrific abuse in detail. In doing so, he would often freeze, convulse, trem-ble, shake, and whisper, while his voice sounded younger. He would jolt, ache, itch, and scream as if he had been bitten by a snake, felt as if he was being buried alive, or was forced to eat human flesh. On leaving the session, he would then go back to his home and put all his memories into a journal; this helped him speed up the recovery process.

A session with Bruce would often begin with him arriving look-ing pale, tired, and unwashed. He would climb up the stairs rapidly, declaring how angry he felt. Within seconds, this would flare up into an explosive rage, shouting and swearing as if his perpetrators were standing next to us. Soon after these extraordi-nary outbursts, his body would display the pain of the abuse: spasms, stiffness, shaking, trembling, remembering episodes where he had regularly been raped, thrown around, bitten, and tortured. I would often hold Bruce through the reliving of the trauma, reas-suring him that that was then and that he is now safe. He would then burst into uncontrollable sobs, wishing he were dead, wishing he were someone else.

One of the many alters/identities was the severely sexually abused child who could only relate through his sexuality. Bruce has named him as "Steve", who can only think of having sex. However, when this finally happened, a suicide ideation would take place, leaving him feeling worse than before. The little boy and the adult Bruce were, and still are, very confused about the issues and boundaries around sex, love, and desire. This meant an intensified erotic countertransference between us. This is still work in progress.

A few months into the therapy, Bruce took a massive risk, something he had not done before in his life; he left a phone message confessing that he loved me. I told him that he is worthy of love, too, but this time it must be modelled to him appropriately in a boundaried way. Little Bruce deserved to be loved in a secure and safe way, and this is what he needs most, and, as his caring therapist, it was my duty to keep this love safe and contained. Bruce felt relieved and lighter after he confided his real feelings to a woman for the first time in his life. This theme still plays a part in our journey, but less so, as little Bruce is developing a real maternal attachment to me and a sense of a core self is emerging. He is able to express excitement as well as mourn something so alien and unfamiliar, but, at the same time, extremely threatening to the old system. Talking about this new set of feelings for the first time in his life was not only overwhelming, but terrifying: how risky they are. How dangerous this must be. What if I am not telling the truth? What if something happens to me? What if I go away and never come back? If attachment means dependency, then attachment is dangerous and unreliable. During one session, while crying, little Bruce told me: this love with boundaries you are modelling to me, is so painful, so strange and unfamiliar, yet feels nice and safe.

One of the prime functions of the infant–mother relationship is to regulate physiological arousal in the infant. Victims of childhood abuse and neglect fail to regulate their arousal levels and need a much higher activation in their brain to feel soothed.

I often find it fascinating how much time of the classical psychoanalytic training is spent on hate and destructiveness in the transference. Not much is mentioned about the terror of love in the clinical setting. Indeed, I often tell my clients, it is much easier to hate than to love.

Bowlby (1998a,b), in his trilogy on separation and loss, wrote, "whenever loss is permanent, as it is after a bereavement, anger and aggressive behaviour are necessarily without function" (p. 286).

Christmas is one of the hardest times for our survivors. It is time when human sacrifice takes place and when our clients were most terrorized and abused. My work with Bruce was intense, yet highly rewarding. I certainly needed a break. We agreed to be in touch online or through text messaging. And, if needed, he would go the Samaritans, with whom he used to be in daily contact before coming to see me. I also left him the number of a couple of helplines. Adult Bruce kindly told me how I deserved a holiday, and so I set off. Unfortunately, in my holiday resort there was no Internet connection, and when I received couple of angry text massages, I responded to him, reassuring him that I would be back soon.

Bowlby, in his writing on disorganized attachment, has noticed that after prolonged separation from the parent, the child will construct a segregated system where both fear and anger are compartmentalized, because any display would be likely to alienate the child still further from their attachment figure.

At our reunion session, Bruce angrily marched into my house not making any eye contact, and as I sat down, there he was, "the Hulk", in all his glory and might, his skin pale, his blue eyes turned brown and narrowed, his eyebrows joined to each other, grinding his teeth and his voice bristling with rage.

"Have you got any idea, have you got any idea what we've been through all by ourselves going through the worst of times, the worst of memories, the worst of hell and without the Samaritans we would be dead, yes, dead! So don't tell me to calm down and take that smirk off your face. I'm asking you: why did you not keep your promise? Have you got any idea what we've been through? You clearly don't, you are clearly another person from the caring therapist to the non-existent person you became. Please stop saying sorry and repeating yourself unless you have a good justification as to why you weren't in touch with us when you promised to be. We have trusted you, relied upon you and you have let us down, you have let us down big time, and I don't know that I want to come back here ever again. This is pathetic, absolutely pathetic!"

My body froze, my neck stiffened, I apologized profusely for not having an Internet connection, and said that I had been thinking of him. Nothing seemed to calm his rage. This went on for forty minutes or so. I suddenly realized that I had to switch off during my holiday, and I shared it with him. His shouting paused, "Finally an honest answer", he angrily exclaimed, and as he was about to leave the room, I, somehow, reached out for a little tortoise souvenir I bought on my holiday and in a tiny voice asked him, "Please stay."

At this point he switched into little Bruce and started to cry. I had to extend the session. Sobbing, Bruce told me about his hellish Christmas, memories around the sacrifice of his little baby brother and how they threatened that they would kill his younger sibling if he did not slash the baby's throat.

During the following months, we would recover more unbearable memories, flashbacks, and nightmares of ritual torture and abuse. The Hulk would appear on a regular basis. He sometimes would start his shouting from the bottom of my street. He would start a session announcing, "There is a lot of rage about today. This time it is against my father." His head turned down as if gathering all his strength for the fight. I would instantly tense up, feeling the terror and dread gradually building inside me. And as his violent shouting took place, the window glass would gently rattle, the air stood still. I would jump and then freeze, feeling totally paralysed by the experience. Each time I'd try to prepare myself, but no amount of preparation would ever make it any easier; on the contrary, the closer our relationship became the more abusive it felt, the harder it became to bear.

Van der Kolk (1989) sees that what needs to be understood is the long-term neurophysiological aspect of PTSD, and the victim's compulsion to repeat the trauma lies at the heart of the traumatic origins of violence.

The Hulk was born when Bruce was nine years old. Prior to the Hulk, there was Leo, who was the first alter to protect Bruce from trusting anyone. Leo would sometimes lash out, kicking an adult who was trying to be nice to little Bruce, warning him that humans are not to be trusted even if they appear to be kind.

For those of you not familiar with the character, the Hulk is cast as the emotional and impulsive alter ego of the withdrawn and reserved physicist, Dr Bruce Banner. The Hulk appears shortly after Banner is accidentally exposed to the blast of a test detonation of a gamma bomb he invented. Subsequently, Banner will involuntarily transform into the Hulk, depicted as a giant, raging, humanoid monster, leading to extreme complications in Banner's life. The

Hulk's creation was inspired by a combination of Dr Jekyll and Mr Hyde and Frankenstein.

Although the Hulk's colouration has varied throughout the character's publication history, the most consistent shade is green. As the Hulk, Banner is capable of significant feats of strength, which increases in direct proportion to the character's anger. Strong emotions, such as anger, terror, and grief are also triggers for forcing Banner's transformation into the Hulk.

Little Bruce's Hulk was born at night, around a solstice date in the satanic calendar, when a big party took place at a large mansion house in the country. Everyone was there—the whole paedophile ring and other familiar faces, all smartly dressed, some wearing masks. Little Bruce knew what was coming, he had had enough, he had nothing to lose, he wanted to die. At this point something very big inside him, someone with a huge voice and uncontained anger, suddenly took over. At the top of the elegant staircase, there he stood in all his might, feeling fearless, free of the abuse, free of all of them, all alone in the world, he screamed the house down: "You f—g, c—s!!!" They all looked shocked and very worried; never before had any child dared to display and protest with such a voice.

The consequence was inevitable: his punishment was due any minute; rape was not enough. They had to upgrade the level of mind control and torture. They had to make sure that the young boy who publicly humiliated them was silenced forever, and so, from the ages of nine to thirteen, my client was exposed to the most horrifying methods of abuse and terror, in which speed, heights, and suicidal mind control were the main tortures. He was nearly drowned, put into dangerous roller-coasters, hung off the top of buildings, placed in fast cars driven through dark tunnels, pushed out of an aeroplane tied to a parachute and permanently injuring his knee, and strapped to the wing of an aeroplane while it was in flight. The Hulk was regularly assaulted, bitten, caged, and imprisoned.

Facing the Hulk for the first nine months was unpleasant, but somehow manageable. However, the greater the attachment that took place, the less safe I felt being in the same room as him. I increasingly felt the dread around his outbursts of rage, whether they were directed at his perpetrators or aimed at me. This reached a climax when, on one occasion, Bruce felt I acted wrongly. He told me that the Hulk was very angry with me, and he slammed down the phone, shouting, "I'll see you tomorrow." At this point, I felt very unsafe being in the same room with Hulk, as there was no reasoning capacity, especially when I was confident that I had not acted wrongly.

I was dreading the confrontation I had to face, and so I called him back, suggesting that we should have a phone session where the Hulk could express his uncontrollable rage at me while I was listening.

"This is exactly why men with my kind of history don't seek therapy and end up in prison or locked into psychiatric units," he angrily responded. "The Hulk needs a safe place to express his rage and you are forbidding him that, you are restricting him. You must not restrict him. I told you he won't harm you; he's been imprisoned long enough. He needs to express himself. He is a big part of me and you are denying us access to your house. Where can we go now? This would only make him more isolated and angry. What is your supervisor's opinion? Maybe you haven't resolved your own issues?"

I listened and agreed with his argument in the main. I then asked him to have an internal conference and try to convey to the Hulk that we are all in this together, trying to find ways of relating to each other, and I know how lonely he is. I told him that I know how he helped Bruce stay alive during his abuse and that the Hulk taught him not to trust anyone, not to fear them, to stand up to them. He had also fought them, and, thanks to him, they stayed alive, all alone, feeling angry and bruised, jailed in a world of mistrust where there was no dialogue, no negotiation, and no relationship. Now that we were doing so well, the majority of Bruce's internal population was seeking proximity to an attachment figure, something that the Hulk was terrified of.

For the following session, Bruce turned up looking contemplative and thoughtful. This was the spokesman for the Hulk. I sat quietly, listening to him advocate the Hulk's position in the system.

"Obviously, he is really hurt by your rejection of him, but we all talked with each other and it is important for you not to judge or criticize him. He is there for a reason, and you need to love him like you love the others, otherwise he'll just get more violent and out of control."

For the next couple of months, the Hulk still appeared around triggering dates. Particularly after Bruce had been rejected, disappointed, or felt needy or humiliated, the Hulk would defend Bruce with his fist and raging voice.

Although this extreme defensive response had served its immediate purpose of protecting the child and adult from unmanageable arousal and trauma, it left the child/adult with little understanding of his own body, emotional makeup, or how to negotiate and survive everyday relationships (Figure 2).

I tried to convey to Bruce that by my not feeling safe, the Hulk was now actually holding back the process of recovery and integration, despite his original good intentions to try to protect little Bruce from getting hurt. As with the entire non-relational group inside the system, the Hulk had internalized the ways and methods of his abusers. His aggressive, frightening gaze must have mirrored Bruce's grandfather and father. His isolation meant no relationship: no reasoning process between two subjects, no negotiation, and certainly no integration. The spokesman insisted that in order for that to shift, the Hulk needed to be convinced that he was accepted and loved.

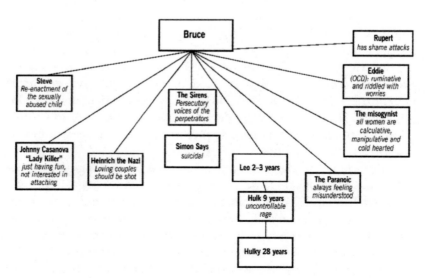

Figure 2. The internal structure of the non-relational group.

As with some female survivors who self harm, releasing tension and anxiety as the Hulk did is a way of gaining control over the experience and the loss. At the neurological level, the brain will experience an analgesic effect through the production of opioid or morphine-like substances. Camila Batmanghelidjh, who works with very traumatized children, claims that as a way of weaning these children from the re-enactment of their trauma, her organization has found constructive ways of releasing the adrenalin in their bodies by taking them to martial arts, rollercoaster rides, and boxing. I also suggested to Bruce that he should go on long runs, or should box a cushion. Unfortunately, this was not of much use to him, as his shoulder had been dislocated as a result of the abuse and he also suffered from ME.

Rage is a response to loss, frozen tears that turn into muscles. Counting up and mourning Bruce's losses is an ongoing process that will take many years to heal. What I feel is taking place at the moment is a continuous dialogue between myself and the spokesperson. A mediation process of reasoning and communication is occurring between me and the rest of the non-relational group. The young ones are very much attached to me and the other creative and relational parts are extremely grateful for the therapy. I feel more comfortable sharing my experiences about the Hulk, how I care and feel for his pain of loneliness, but at the same time how unhelpful I become to him when he shouts and I resort to a basic human response of freeze/fight/flight.

The spokesperson told me that negotiation with the Hulk was currently taking place. The system has realized that what the Hulk gets out of his shouting is a sense of control and empowerment. He managed to convey to him, "Look, we already won, there is no need to lash out at people in the present who love and care for us". As this healthy dialogue was taking place, I found myself naming him "Hulky". We also decided to release him from his internal prison and give him a nice, comfortable room. This has really helped to make a difference; the spokesman informed me that he likes his new room and name.

When Hulky eventually left the room, depression crept up on Bruce, and little Bruce came twitching in his eyes, whispering with a younger voice, "I am all alone in the house, Hulk really helped me." Coming back from that regressive state, Bruce looked at me, and said that he thinks he is ready to let go of him now. He wished we could have some kind of ceremony for the Hulk's service and departure. The following sessions were riddled with heavy sadness; Bruce looked broken and stricken by an intense grief, feeling of depression, and suicidal ideation. The spokesman tearfully told me, "If Hulk leaves, Bruce will have to be in touch with the unbearable feelings of despair, sadness, loss, and even suicide. Expressing his murderous rage was a way of gaining control over his grief."

A week later, I received a phone call from Bruce, telling me that he had spotted one of his abusers seated in a restaurant with some other people. In a shockingly calm manner, he first confirmed the man's name, then confronted him by calling him a rapist in front of the other diners. The man looked pale and shocked, while Bruce marched out, not believing what he had just done.

Marking this as an act of bravery and a breakthrough of our good work with the Hulk, I bought Bruce toy figurine of the Hulk with a Bruce Banner doll inside him. We congratulated the Hulk's progress towards integration, modelling this huge step forward from aggression to assertion.

De Zulueta (1993), quoting Van der Kolk, wrote that working with people who have been traumatized confronts therapists as well as patients with intense emotional experiences. It forces them to explore the darkest corners of the mind, and to face the entire spectrum of human glory and degradation. Sooner or later, these experiences have the potential to overwhelm therapists. The repeated exposure to their own vulnerability becomes too intense, the display of the infinite human capacity for cruelty too unbearable, the enactment of the trauma within the therapeutic relationship too terrifying.

It is just over a year now since I first met Hulky. Currently, whenever Bruce experiences anger during the session, I listen to my countertransference. It is no longer a feeling of dread that comes between us, but a human feeling of irritation, frustration, assertion, and anger, but no longer to the extent of feeling unsafe.

If I ask him how Hulky is, he closes his eyes and, after couple of minutes, he reports back, "He is OK, he is still feeling excluded in the main, but he is listening."

Unfortunately, for centuries, men have been permitted to be violent, while with most female survivors of ritual abuse, an internal

Hulk would be most likely to have expressed itself through self-harm. Working with male survivors of sexual, ritual, and sadistic abuse can naturally bring the potential to feel unsafe within the consulting room. Therefore, the number one priority is to create a safe space for both therapist and client. Now that we have paved the way for me and for Bruce to work safely, we can continue working with all the many relational and non-relational part-selves inside him.

Bowlby (1998a), in his volume on separation about children who had been separated from their care-givers, found that when the conditions of separation were prolonged and stressful, the behaviour observed upon reunion was detached, cut-off, disconnected, and bewildered, with gaze aversion .

On our reunion after the summer vacation, Bruce was in a bad place, having been triggered and disappointed by a relationship with a girl he met over his holiday, and so Hulky was around. "There is a lot of rage inside and I don't know what to do with it."

Listening to my countertransference, I felt the dread creeping up, but without the same velocity, and so I said to him, "What would you like to do? Is it Hulky?"

At this point, he shrugged his shoulders, looking distant and detached. For the first time since I had met him, he went into a forty-minute silence, crying and wanting to be left alone.

When I finally managed to get a response out of him, he then manically switched into hysterical laughter. When he finally calmed down, I asked, "Was that Hulky?" He then cheekily replied, "I think his name now is SULKY!"

These are still early days in therapy, and we still have a long way to go. The dialogues with the spokesperson are still ongoing, and so whenever Hulky turns up he is there for brief moments. I find that the spokesperson that communicates and mediates Hulky's position is not only inspiring, but is also a sign of hope. This hope does not only belong to Bruce and Hulky, but to many other severely abused men who are terrified of seeking therapy.

Working with survivors of ritual abuse can be challenging on so many levels: not only do we enter the survivor's world of terror, helplessness, and loneliness, but we also have to put up with facing the denial in the wider society that these things are happening. It is, therefore, important never to lose hope; after all, what is the meaning of life if we do not face a battle that is bigger than us?

References

Bowlby, J. (1998a). *Attachment & Loss*: Volume 2, *Separation, Anger and Anxiety*. London: Pimlico.

Bowlby, J. (1998b). *Attachment & Loss*: Volume 3, *Loss, Sadness and Depression*. London: Pimlico.

De Zulueta, F. (1993). *From Pain to Violence*. London: Whurr.

van der Kolk, B. A. (1989). The compulsion to repeat the trauma: re-enactment, revictimization, and masochism. *Psychiatric Clinics of North America, 12*(2): 389–411.

CHAPTER SIX

Maintaining agency: a therapist's journey

Sue Richardson

Professional journey 1966–1988

My professional journey started when I entered social work in 1966. By specializing in child care and family work, I became a *de facto* specialist in child abuse and protection. In 1986, I was appointed by Cleveland Social Services Department as their Child Abuse Consultant, a post created in the wake of a high profile public inquiry into the death of Jasmine Beckford (HMSO, 1985). I was given a strong political and professional mandate to tackle child abuse, and I was filled with a sense of agency. Together with the paediatricians, Marietta Higgs and Geoffrey Wyatt, I was a key figure in the 1987 Cleveland child abuse crisis, when what was then an unprecedented number of children were medically diagnosed as having suffered sexual abuse. Our efforts to bring this to attention and to protect the children precipitated a public outcry of disbelief, orchestrated by the media and one local MP, and led to the Butler-Sloss Inquiry.

The Butler-Sloss Inquiry was a breakthrough in societal awareness of sexual abuse summed up by the opening of its conclusion:

We have learnt during the Inquiry that sexual abuse occurs in children of all ages, including the very young, to boys as well as girls, in all classes of society and frequently within the family. The sexual abuse can be very serious and on occasions includes vaginal, anal and oral intercourse. [Butler-Sloss, 1988, p. 243]

At the same time, I regard the inquiry report as a political document used to calm disquiet, contain the extent of the emerging problem, and inform procedural solutions. It was not within its brief to determine whether or not the children had been abused. It did not analyse child abuse as a phenomenon, and decided against hearing expert evidence about behaviour of perpetrators. Neither did it respond to all the data submitted by myself and my colleagues concerning children trapped in silence. Instead, it focused on the management of those children who are able to make a disclosure and take part in a child protection investigation. A different analysis of Cleveland from the perspective of gender-based politics is provided by Campbell (1997). A different professional analysis and the data on the children were published by those of us at the centre of events (Richardson & Bacon, 1991).

Butler-Sloss (1988) expressed the hope that all of us who had been involved would be able to work together for the good of children in Cleveland. I was very keen to do this and take forward what I had learnt, but, along with my paediatric colleagues, I was treated as the bearer of an unwanted message. My much-heralded post of Child Abuse Consultant was declared redundant. I faced the collapse of my professional networks and career in child protection and had to find another way to maintain my sense of personal and professional agency.

Outcomes of the Cleveland journey

The personal and professional outcomes of Cleveland have been permanent for me and are an integral part of my current work with ritual abuse. To paraphrase Bowlby (1988), I was left knowing what I am not supposed to know and feeling what I am not supposed to feel. I was acutely aware of the lost narratives of the majority of abused children and adults, who also know what they were not supposed to know and feel what they are not supposed to feel, and I developed a rising awareness of dissociation as a way of understanding where some of their lost narratives had gone.

I have never become immune to the emotional impact of abuse, but, at the height of the Cleveland crisis, after a day spent trying to manage the influx of children diagnosed by the paediatricians as having suffered sexual abuse, I used to go home thinking that at least I had heard the worst of what can happen to children, only to hear of yet more the next day. So, I developed a degree of affective tolerance. I learnt then that there is no end to the varieties of savagery which adults can inflict on children and never to think that I had heard it all.

As Herman (1992) says, moral neutrality in response to trauma is not useful, and being a bystander was never an option for me. This stance has implications. I was exposed to the savagery of denial and scapegoating in an unsupportive and hostile professional and political context, with all its spin and distortion. I regard these as fear-driven systems that affect entire professional networks to this day. Struggling for support, I slowly realized that the decision to hold on to my sense of agency was essentially down to me.

Repair of agency

In making the paradigm shift to understanding the significance of child abuse in the aetiology of trauma and dissociation, I created a two-edged sword, because it was both the cause of my difficulties and also the source of my agency. At the same time, I found this preferable to dissociating from what I had learnt, a strategy I felt some of the colleagues I left behind in social work had resorted to.

I carried on care-seeking and found that any crumbs of care-giving can go a long way. What I needed care-giving for, beyond mere survival, was to enable me to process my experiences. I cannot overemphasize the value of taking time to do this as key to remaining open to the emotional content of others' traumatic experiences without loss of agency via vicarious traumatization. My peer group fragmented and the absence of professional care-giving was appalling (Richardson & Bacon, 2001a). My resources expanded when I became one of the first intake in the psychotherapy training provided by what is now the Bowlby Centre. This gave me the opportunity to process the emotional impact of events and somehow keep both my left and right brains functioning. With the support of John Southgate and Kate White, I did much grieving and mourning: weeping and wailing, expressing anger, and confronting despair.

I was determined to bear witness rather than be silenced, and to get the lost narrative of Cleveland's children heard. I spoke at a large number of conferences and meetings and published two books with my colleagues (Richardson & Bacon, 1991, 2001b) and several papers.

I had some allies in other beleaguered colleagues and adult survivors. I knew nothing at that time of ritual abuse, and only opened my mind to it after meeting with colleagues from the Broxstowe case in Nottingham. In this case, professionals were at first commended by the High Court for protecting a group of children from sadistic abuse, but were subsequently derided in the media and elsewhere for believing the children's further disclosures, which were replete with indicators of satanic ritual abuse. These colleagues drew attention to the possible significance of some of the drawings published in our account of Cleveland's children. For example, a child who was seen by a clinical psychologist drew her abuser dressed as a devil figure (Richardson & Bacon, 1991, p. 117). While it has never been established whether or not this child or any of the children in Cleveland had suffered ritual abuse, some professionals are now of the opinion that this may have been a factor in the crisis.

I did not anticipate it on moving into psychotherapy, but into the therapeutic space stepped adult survivors of ritual abuse, daring to believe that I might be prepared to hear of experiences similar to this child's drawing. I began to see the potential significance in what some of my clients drew, such as an all-seeing eye or an inverted crucifix, or spoke of, such as memories of robed figures and chanting. One of these clients had a vivid implicit memory of what presented as ritual abuse ceremonies, which she was able to draw very clearly but without any conscious memory of them at all. I started to get an idea of what it is like for clients to live with a loss of agency in everyday life, and I was on a steep learning curve.

Professional learning curve

My journey alongside survivors of ritual abuse has shown me that there are two kinds of dissociation to consider. First, clinical dissociation as the sequelae of disorganized attachment and interpersonal trauma. In this instance, any sense of agency tends to be fragmented and held by different parts. The second kind, deliberately induced dissociation, is the sequelae of the use of terror designed to maintain the perpetrator's power and control and, by its nature, is more undermining of agency. That profound loss of agency is illustrated by a survivor or ritual abuse who said, "It bothers me that I don't know how to exist. I don't know how to BE, unless it is to someone else's design. I can't find me. There is nothing there. I can't answer questions about what I want because I don't know how to locate 'I'."

As a result of the way in which abusers manipulate attachment needs, the whole concept of relationship is problematic to the survivor and all the notions we hold dear as therapists are seen as dangerous. For example, the more caring the therapeutic relationship is and the more it develops, the more the expectation increases that it is a precursor to abuse and a part inside gives the message to flee. As a result, I find I am often seen by clients as highly suspect when I relate in a kind and friendly manner.

My learning curve has led me to develop what one of my clients has called a "methodology of healing" as a framework for practice. It is influenced by a new attachment paradigm developed by Heard, Lake, and McCluskey (2009). Devising my own methodology using attachment theory has been very empowering for me and my clients, and seems to achieve lift-off in therapy for those who can use it.

In summary, I have identified an "internal attachment system" with patterns of internal care-seeking–care-giving as a key target of intervention (Richardson, 2010). I find that helping to build an internal attachment hierarchy can be more viable and less threatening than an emphasis on relationship with the therapist. I see my role as being what Blizard (2003) calls a "relational bridge" for the parts inside. Some parts can be brilliant care-givers; for example, knowing how to manage avoidant parts who are terrified of proximity by keeping a tolerable distance, giving just the right amount of reassurance or using other child parts to make an alliance with terrified inner children. I have reframed questions from the Adult Attachment Interview (AAI) into an "internal attachment interview" (Richardson, 2010). The quality of the narrative sheds light on internal attachment patterns, provides a map of internal relational configurations, and identifies tasks of repair.

Some ongoing challenges to therapeutic agency

To act as a relational bridge in a way which supports the growth of internal care-seeking and care-giving means attuning to multiple feeling states, attachment styles, and developmental stages. For example, one client asked each part of her system what they thought of me. Some parts did not know to whom she was referring, and it had to be explained that I am the person they see on the same day at same time every week. Another part thought they just might recognize me by my characteristic appearance. Yet another part said dismissively that they know perfectly well who I was, but could take me or leave me alone. In addition, as in every system, there were traumatized children desperately seeking attachment.

Evolving strategies to deal with the effects of programming designed to destabilize or destroy attachments is challenging and just beginning. More challenging still is bearing witness to a history of atrocity, one in which the client may have been forced to take part. The nature of this, along with the client's dysregulated care-seeking, arouses our own care-giving systems. Care-givers would normally reach their goal when well-being has been restored in the care-seeker. However, clients who have suffered ritual abuse can have immense difficulty in reaching the goal of well-being. I find I am often faced by chronic, unassuaged care-seeking by distressed parts and poor, absent, or punitive internal care-giving. This can be quite dysregulating for me as a professional care-giver. I suspect it is the source of potential therapeutic hazards that are all too easy to judge in our peers, such as loss of boundaries.

Journey to date: maintaining agency

In my experience, it makes a lot of difference to belong to professional organizations and networks such as the European Society for

Dissociation and its UK network, the special interest group on ritual abuse and mind control set up by the International Society for the Study of Trauma and Dissociation, and small peer groups. This reduces isolation and helps to maintain vitality through interest sharing.

In the wake of Cleveland, I have learnt to live with conflicting and incoherent narratives at every level (Richardson, 2008). In individual therapeutic work, I am regularly afflicted by doubt that not everything is what it seems, and have become aware that the system is not always right. I know I have been misled at times by parts who are still relying on old ways to survive. In response, I try to see the journey as a shared search with the client for their "reality" and "truth" and the construction of a narrative that is sufficiently coherent to live by.

For sources of inspiration, among other things I draw on poetry (e.g., Jennings, 1986; Nightingale, 1988) and literature (e.g., Slovo, 2000). I share these resources with clients when appropriate, as they do with me when creative writing and poetry is part of exploratory therapy.

I hold on to hope for healing. From an attachment perspective, hope can be informed by the client undoing any belief in the perpetrators as the sole source of care; recognizing that attachment to the perpetrators cannot provide what other relationships can; seeing all parts of the self as worthy of care rather than as "evil" or culpable, and co-creating a means of effective internal care-seeking and care-giving. It is my experience that survivors of ritual abuse and mind control can restructure their internal care-seeking and care-giving and move from an insecure internal world to one which is more secure.

I find that engaging in exploration, creative "play", and symbolic communication is part of the upside of my work. I have a small collection of toys in my therapy room (Figure 1), along with paints, clay, storybooks, and various symbolic objects which adult clients often use to work on restructuring their internal attachment systems. As the internal relational structure represented in toys or other materials changes, the narrative also changes. Then the toys and materials are no longer needed and are put away or bequeathed to my collection, which, for this reason, is growing.

Figure 1.   Toys used in my therapy room.

Journey from 1987 to the present date: conclusions

In conclusion, I can affirm that agency is tenacious, both in myself as a professional after times of deep despair, and in even the most apparently damaged clients, for whom allowing themselves to remember what they are supposed to forget is a huge act of agency in itself.

On my journey to date, I have seen the wheel come full circle. The proactive assertive approach to child protection for which we were condemned in Cleveland has been called for in subsequent cases of child deaths elsewhere, such as Baby P, killed at age two.

Even though previous crises in Nottingam, Rochdale, and Orkney were shut down, ritual abuse keeps trying to emerge. Dare we hope that ritual abuse will have its Cleveland, which will bring about a paradigm shift in its understanding and recognition? Dare we hope for a genuine discourse and an end to multiple and conflicting states of mind about knowing *vs.* not knowing about forms of ritual abuse and mind control? My journey so far has not given me the answer to these questions. I hold on to a vision for the future of a changed societal and professional context that provides for the unfolding of unheard narratives and recognizes and supports the complex and challenging tasks of repair and witness to survivors of ritual abuse. For this to happen, all of us have to take on the burden of change with its potential rewards. The endeavour is a political one, and its nature transformational. The challenge and rewards are summed up by a survivor as follows:

When I think of the generations gone
When I think of the generations gone to darkness
When I think of the generations gone to madness
It makes me shudder.

Out of nowhere but the infinity of space
    and eternity of time
Out of the deep, deep ground with its hidden secrets
This revelation was flung to us

To be the generations that bring truth into the light
To be the last bearers of that trembling of the mind
To be the first who speak of the violation of the body

Tremble, space
Tremble, time
We come with the truth of mans' bearing
Of nature's desperate clawing at the night
We come with the burden of change on us
With the shifting of consciousness's tectonic plates
We come holding Utopia
In the guise of the unmentionable

Wreathed in atrocity we bring the sunrise
Of women's and men's potential
We carry new dynasties in dung stained hands

We, the lucky unlucky ones
We, the dirt under your feet
Bring you the future

An equable humanity
Free from the consequences of man's lust. [Evans, 2006, p. 5]

References

Blizard, R. A. (2003). Disorganised attachment, development of dissociated self states, and a relational approach to treatment. *Journal of Trauma and Dissociation*, 4(3): 27–50.

Bowlby, J. (1988). On knowing what you are not supposed to know and feeling what you are not supposed to feel. In: *A Secure Base* (pp. 99–118). London: Routledge.

Butler-Sloss, Rt Hon Justice E. (1988). *Report of the Inquiry into Child Abuse in Cleveland 1987*. London: HMSO.

Campbell, B. (1997). *Unofficial Secrets – Child Sexual Abuse: The Cleveland Case* (2nd edn). London: Virago.

Evans, K. (2006). *Journey into Healing*. London: Survivor's Press.

Heard, D., Lake, H., & McCluskey, U. (2009). *Attachment Therapy for Adults and Adolescents: Theory and Practice Post-Bowlby*. London: Karnac.

Herman, J. L. (1992). *Trauma and Recovery*. New York: Basic Books.

HMSO (1985). *A Child in Trust: Report of the Panel of Inquiry into the Circumstances Surrounding the Death of Jasmine Beckford*. London: HMSO.

Nightingale, C. (1988). *Journey of a Survivor*. Bristol: Constance Nightingale.

Jennings, E. (1986). *Collected Poems*. Manchester: Carcanet.

Richardson, S. (2008). Cleveland 20 years on: themes of disruption and repair in the trauma narratives of children, adults and society. *Child Abuse Review, 17*: 230–241.

Richardson, S. (2010). Reaching for relationship: exploring the use of an attachment paradigm in the assessment and repair of the dissociative internal world. *Attachment: New Directions in Psychotherapy and Relational Psychoanalysis, 4*: 7–25.

Richardson, S., & Bacon, H. (Eds.) (1991). *Child Sexual Abuse: Whose Problem? Reflections from Cleveland*. Birmingham: Venture Press.

Richardson, S., & Bacon, H. (2001a). Piecing the fragments together. In: S. Richardson & H. Bacon (Eds.), *Creative Responses to Child Sexual Abuse: Challenges and Dilemmas* (pp. 29–43). London: Jessica Kingsley.

Richardson, S. & Bacon, H. (Eds.) (2001b). *Creative Responses to Child Sexual Abuse: Challenges and Dilemmas*. London: Jessica Kingsley.

Slovo, G. (2000). *Red Dust*. London: Virago.

INDEX